Pan-Africanism in Barbados

www.ingramcontent.com/pod-product-compliance
Lightning Source LLC
Chambersburg PA
CBHW022112280326
41933CB00007B/358

Pan-Africanism in Barbados

An Analysis of the Activities of the Major
20th-Century Pan-African Formations
in Barbados

Rodney Worrell

New Academia Publishing, LLC
Washington, DC

Printed in the United States of America

Library of Congress Control Number: 2004116606
ISBN 0-9744934-6-5 paperback

New Academia Publishing, LLC
P.O. Box 27420, Washington, DC 20038-7420
www.newacademia.com - info@newacademia.com

This book is dedicated to my late brother and comrade Ryan O'Neal Scantlebury, I am proud that you were flesh of my flesh and blood of my blood. This book is also dedicated to all the Barbadian Pan-African warriors, who have fought and are still fighting for the betterment and dignity of the African masses in Barbados.

Contents

Preface

Each generation must, out of relative obscurity, discover its mission, fulfill it or betray it. In underdeveloped countries the preceding generations have both resisted the work of erosion carried out by colonialism and also helped on the maturing of the struggles today. We must rid ourselves of the habit, now that we are in the thick of the fight, of minimizing the action of our fathers or of feigning incomprehension when considering their silence and passivity. They fought as well as they could, with the arms that they possessed then; and if the echoes of their struggle have not resounded in the international arena, we must realize that the reason for this silence lies less in their lack of heroism than in the fundamentally different situation of our time. It needed more than one native to say 'We've had enough'; more than one peasant revolt rising crushed, more than one demonstration put down before we could today hold our own, certain in our victory. As for us who have decided to break the back of colonialism, our historic mission is to sanction all revolts, all desperate actions, all those abortive attempts drowned in rivers of blood.
-Frantz Fanon, *The Wretched of the Earth*

This book sets out to fulfill a long felt need for a work on Pan-Africanism in Barbados. To my knowledge this is the first attempt at writing a narrative on Pan-Africanism within the Barbadian context. Additionally, it seeks to demonstrate that Pan-Africanism in Barbados has a long historiography as a method of resistance, struggle and survival.

From 1636 when Africans were first brought to Barbados as slaves, a form of proto-Pan-Africanism existed among them. This proto-Pan-Africanism was manifested in many different forms of protestation:

- The aborted attempts at rebellion in 1649, 1675,1692 and 1701,
- Attempts at maronage, and all forms of resisting the system of slavery and Western dominance,
- A form of proto-Pan-Africanism was also evident in the 1816 rebellion when the enslaved Africans wanted to overthrow the slave system and take their freedom.

Therefore, from the beginning of the African experience in Barbados, Pan-Africanism in its diverse and varied forms has always had one central thread, the betterment of the condition of the African masses.

The first chapter establishes the theoretical framework for this study and seeks to educate the reader as to what is Pan-Africanism. Chapter two examines the Universal Negro Improvement Association and the Workings Men Association — two Garveyite organizations. Chapter three looks at the Pan-African figures that sought to give leadership to the mass of workers in the turbulent period of 1937. In the following chapter this writer places the Peoples Progressive Movement/ *Black Star* newspaper under the microscope as they sought to engage in the neo-colonial struggle. Chapter five analyses the Black Nights, Southern Africa Liberation Committee, the Rastafarian Movement, Marcus Garvey Committee, Clement Payne Movement and the Pan-African Movement of Barbados.

My first attempt at writing on the Pan-African project in Barbados occurred when I wrote my undergraduate Caribbean Studies thesis, "The Pan-African Influence in the 1937 Barbadian Revolt"; this work excited me and forced me to delve further in the wider currents of Pan-Africanism in my masters' thesis. The study examined some of the challenges of global Pan-Africanism and continental Pan-Africanism in the new conjuncture of capitalist expansionism/internationalization without looking at Pan-Africanism in Barbados. Dr. Neville Duncan (my M.Phil. thesis supervisor), Dr. Don Marshal and Dr. Glenford Howe literally coerced me to write a chapter on "Pan-Africanism in Barbados", for their publication *The Empowering Impulse: The Nationalist Tradition of Barbados*. Dr. Duncan after reading the chapter suggested that I should write a book on Pan-Africanism in Barbados. I was not so inclined, but after presenting the findings of my research at a public seminar held under the auspices of the Pan-African Movement of Barbados, there was a general outcry for such a work. Therefore, after successfully writing an M.Phil. thesis, several chapters, seminar presentations, and articles in academic journals on Pan-Africanism, I believed that I should take up the challenge and write this work.

I owe a fraternal debt to Dr. Neville Duncan, Dr. Richard Goodridge, Dr. Tony Phillips, Dr. Don Marshall, Dr. Glenford Howe, Dr. Viola Davis, Trevor Prescod, Kofi Akobi, Glenroy Straughn, Bobby Clarke, Ikael Tafari, David Stanton, Wolde Prescod, Mark Seale, Mark Adamson, Ricky Parris, Michael Cummins, David Commissiong, Joy Workman, Lloyd Jones, David Denny, John Howell, Tony Reid and Dr. David Browne. These individuals provided the intellectual training, information, inspiration, and encouragement to complete this work. I also wish to express my sincerest gratitude to the helpful staff at the Archives, the staff of the University of the West Indies Library, the Public Library and the Library at the Nation newspaper and the Commission for Pan-African Affairs. I will also like to thank Alexandria Jules and Viola Davis for their editorial comments. Special thanks to Gail Clarke for the layout work, and cover design of the first edition.

1
Theoretical Framework

Theoretical framework

This study examines the activities of the major socio-political Pan-African formations that have existed in Barbados during the twentieth-century. Therefore, this study limits itself to an examination of the Pan-African organizations which fit the above criteria. While there have been many other Pan-African religious and cultural bodies it is not the task of this writer to examine these organizations in this work. It is important to note that all the socio-political Pan-African formations that have always existed in the Caribbean have existed as sub-cultural movements. Throughout the Caribbean, social and political movements as sub-cultural manifestations of constant pressure for change have played crucial roles in the social and political development of the Caribbean.[1]

From the middle of the nineteenth century behaviorists have tended to discuss social movements as:

1. vehicles of change;
2. disruptive social forces;
3. manifestations of abnormal psychology; and
4. threats to the status quo.[2]

However, the factor of social change is central to the study of social movements. Sociologists tend to view social movements as reactions to the structural changes in society. They believe that social movements are influenced by technological innovations, economics and population shifts. Therefore, sociologists see social movements as an inevitable consequence of the structural strains within a system.[3]

Many other social scientists view social movements as manifestations of individual needs or discontent. Hans Toch stated: "For the psychologist, these kinds of efforts (social movements) must be monitored. They must stem from specific situations in which they find themselves."[4] Further, Allen Edwards mentions:

> The supporters of any movement, it is true, tend to come from those groups which are already frustrated or anticipate frustration in some respect and which see this particular movement as a means of restoring equilibrium or obtaining relief for their anxiety.[5]

Gary Rush and Sergie Denisoff defines a social movement as a joint organized endeavor of a considerable group of persons, who try in some way to change or alter the course of events by their joint activities.[6] Therefore, the Pan-African formations that existed and the ones still in existence are essentially social movements seeking to realize change locally and internationally. Moreover, Pan-Africanism has always been seen as some fringe activity, and many Pan-Africanists were seen and are still viewed as madmen, social misfits and persons with a disruptive agenda, to be viewed with some degree of suspicion.

What is Pan-Africanism?

The question of what exactly is Pan-Africanism has challenged many scholars and Pan-African activists to provide an adequate working definition. Indeed, Immanuel Geiss contends that it was difficult, perhaps even impossible, to provide a clear definition of Pan-Africanism.[7] According to Geiss, Pan-Africanism covers:

1. Intellectual and political movements among Africans and Afro-Americans who regard or have regarded Africans and the people of African descent as homogenous. This outlook leads to a feeling of racial solidarity and a new awareness, and causes Afro-Americans to look upon Africa as their real homeland without necessarily thinking of a physical return to Africa;
2. All ideas, which have stressed or sought the cultural unity and political independence of Africa, including the desire to modernize Africa on the basis of equal rights. The key concepts have been respectively the redemption of Africa for the Africans;
3. Ideas or political movements, which have advocated or advocate the political unity of Africa or at least close collaboration in one form or another.[8]

Colin Legum the Pan-African writer shares Geiss' sentiments about the impossibility of providing an adequate definition of Pan-Africanism. He opines that although it is possible to talk about the way Pan-Africanism expresses itself, it is not so easy to give a concise definition of the concept.[9] He stated that Pan-Africanism is:

Essentially a movement of ideas and emotions, at times it achieves a synthesis, at times it remains at the level of thesis and antithesis. In one sense Pan-Africanism can be likened to world federation, Atlantic Union or Federated Europe—each allows for great scope of interpretation in its practical application. And yet in its deepest sense, Pan-Africanism is different from all of these movements in that it is exclusive.[10]

Similarly, Ofutey-Kodjoe suggests that:

Pan-Africanism existed as a body of ideas that led to the formation of a political movement containing many different organizations. These organizations have two common characteristics: the acceptance of a oneness of all African people and a commitment to the betterment of all people of African descent.[11]

Esedebe defines Pan-Africanism as a political and cultural phenomenon, which regards Africa, Africans and African descendants abroad as a unit. It seeks to regenerate and unify Africa and promote a feeling of oneness among the people of the African World. Pan-Africanism glorifies the African past and inculcates pride in African values.[12] Tony Martin defines Pan-Africanism as attempts by African peoples to link up their struggles for their mutual benefits.[13] Judith Stein describes Pan-Africanism as a complex and imprecisely, if passionately held set of racial beliefs joined together to defend and advance black equality and progress. It was a modern blue print for achieving racial equality through economic, technological, social and political developments of all areas where black people lived.[14]

Eusi Kwayana the Pan-African activist seems to have captured the essence of Pan-Africanism in the definition below:

…as a body of thought and action, shared but not uniform or dogmatic. A dynamic movement continually transforming itself and gaining new ideological perspectives in light of changing circumstance. Enriching itself through its own experience. Flowing from mass groups and occasionally members of governments. Tending to the goal of the restoration of freedom and dignity for Africans at home and abroad.[15]

This writer defines Pan-Africanism as a movement and an ideology of African peoples globally, which is concerned with the social, political, economic and psychological upliftment, as well as the protection of Africa and African peoples worldwide. The psychological unity in the struggle of all persons of African ancestry and the organic unification of the African continent are necessary ingredients to the realization of the noble objectives of Pan-Africanism.[16]

The seeds of Pan-Africanism were sown from Africa's incorporation into the capitalist world economy during the first major wave of capitalist internationalization in the sixteenth century. The sixteenth century marked the beginning of regular trade between Europe and other nations. This system was based on the capitalist mode of production. Capitalism from its humble beginnings always had expansionist objectives to satisfy its accumulative appetite. This expansionist ethic led to the geographical expansion of the world economy. The expansion of the sixteenth century was not only a geographical expansion, but also a period of rapid population growth, increased agricultural production and the first industrial revolution. The economic, demographic and industrial expansion pushed the capitalist boundaries outward. These factors led to the development of the plantation system in the Americas. However, there was insufficient labor within the European countries to fully exploit the new tracts of land. The indigenous Amerindians were not suited to the regimented plantation labor and were quickly decimated. Therefore, the capitalist countries turned to Africa to supply the labor that was needed.[17]

The trans-Atlantic slave trade led to the largest and longest coerced migration in recorded history. Moreover, the trans-Atlantic slave trade provided the stimuli that ignited a Pan-African consciousness in the African Diaspora. According to Tony Martin:

> Pan-Africanism became inevitable with the inception of the transatlantic slave trade. Europe by scattering Africa to the winds, inevitably if unwittingly set in motion a process which would bring scattered Africa together again at a higher level. It was inevitable that the forcibly uprooted Africans would yearn to rediscover their homeland. It was inevitable that a final reunification of scattered Africa would come only at the expense of colonial Europe. Thus

was set in motion by the trans-Atlantic slave trade a process
whose course, even now has not fully run.[18]

In the pre-transatlantic slave trade period the Africans placed
great attachment on their respective political groupings (e.g.
Hausa, Ibo, Ashanti, and Yoruba). However, with the development
of the trans-Atlantic slave trade for obvious reasons these political
identities quickly disappeared or became insignificant. European
chattel slavery destroyed the traditional allegiances of the past
by altering a man's or woman's conception of themselves, as
belonging to their ethnic group. Political identities became less
important and the idea of Pan-Africanism began to take root. The
exilic Africans came to the harsh realization that they were now
part of an international community of black people who came
from different countries in Africa, but who now shared a common
experience of slavery, racism and racial discrimination. Therefore,
it was imperative that the Africans would have to unite, and link
up their struggles if they were to be successful in their efforts to
resist their enslavement by whatever means. Slavery became the
basis for racial solidarity, something that did not exist in traditional
Africa where unity was linked to ethnic grouping.[19]

European racism was also an important factor that gave rise
to the emergence of a Pan-African consciousness. The ideology of
racism was developed and systematically applied to legitimize the
enslavement of the Africans. Racism was the ideological couplet
of capitalist expansionism during the first and second wave of
capitalist expansionism. The ideologies of racism devalued the
cultural traits of the Africans, (his/her speech, religious mannerism
and institution forms). These were said to be marks of savagery
and a lower civilization and the denigration was done to deprive
Africans of a sense of collective worth. It is quite clear that the
ideology of racism was used to legitimize African slavery and
was much more all encompassing and all embracing than that
used against the Amerindians. Indeed, the racist attacks on the
physical, genetic and biological attributes of African people, the
color of the African skin, as well as the characteristics of the mouth,

nose, and hair texture, were deemed as symbols of inferiority. The reasons behind extending the ideology from cultural to physical characteristics was to ensure that the African, no matter how successful in assimilating white culture would always remain a "Negro" and by definition a slave. Thus, the "African would remain the subject of unmitigated exploitation and a source of primitive capital accumulation."[20]

The ideology of racism was an attendant to capitalist expansionism during the conversion period. Racism was used to justify the military conquest of Africa and used to buttress the system of colonialism in Africa and the Caribbean. At the turn of the twentieth century the socio-economic condition of African peoples globally had not changed considerably. Indeed, African peoples were still at the bottom of the socio-economic ladder and still suffered from tremendous racial discrimination. The expanding capitalist system was still placing considerable strains on Africans worldwide.

Dennis Benn is of the view that the development of doctrines of black consciousness is firmly rooted in the socio-historical experiences of the African in the Diaspora. He asserts that the growth and development of this doctrine cannot be properly understood without the historical factors that have shaped the black experience in the region.[21] In the Caribbean the large scale introduction of African slaves to provide the labor for the plantation under a dominant minority, produced a social stratification of West Indian society in which the African was excluded from political power, held a low economic status and was at the bottom of the social ladder. The separation of the African from his homeland and his exposure to the cultural practices of the economically and socially dominant white minority subjected him to a number of acculturative pressures seeking to reshape his cultural identity. These factors have produced three basic consequences for the black population in the West Indies, in the form of economic dispossession, social and political deprivation, and cultural disorientation, which have remained fairly constant features of the African condition in the West Indian socio-political order. Benn argued that in a sense doctrines of black consciousness might be seen essentially as intellectual responses to one or more aspects of this condition.[22]

Throughout the colonial world, the immediate post World War 1 period was one of intense ferment. Marcus Garvey and his Universal Negro Improvement Association (UNIA) contributed immensely to the heightened black consciousness and new awareness of African peoples at this juncture. Marcus Garvey started the UNIA movement in Jamaica in 1914. Tony Martin, the Garveyite scholar is of the view that "Garvey was the most potent force for forging a spirit of Pan-African oneness among black people everywhere."[23] Indeed, UNIA branches were created wherever African peoples were found.

Marcus Garvey is the father of twentieth century Black Nationalism. The climate of slavery and racism, which led to African consciousness and racial solidarity, were the primary ingredients that led to the creation of African Nationalism/Black Nationalism. In the Americas, Pan-Africanism has generally been associated with Black Nationalism. Black Nationalism like other forms of nationalism resulted from the desire of a subject people to break away from foreign rule, and to unite traditionally disunited peoples. The ideological reason for nationalism is the notion that the people are tied to a geographical region which they have either traditionally possessed or hope to possess. The national group is seen as being organically connected by language. However, Black Nationalism is unique in that its adherents are not united by a common geography nor a common language, but by the concept of racial unity. Black Nationalism has sometimes, but not always, been concerned with the quest for a nation in the geographical sense. It has been nationalism only because it seeks to unite the entire black family, assuming that the African race has a collective destiny and message for humanity comparable to that of a nation. The essence of Black Nationalism is the feeling on the part of black people that they are responsible for the welfare of other black people as a collective entity because of a shared racial heritage and destiny.[24] Stokeley Carmichael stated that

'Black Nationalism is African Nationalism, which finds its highest aspiration in Pan-Africanism'.[25] Indeed, in many respects Black Nationalism is synonymous with Pan-Africanism especially in the African Diaspora.

Black Nationalism can be seen as a counter movement away from subordination to independence through refutation, to self-affirmation. Black Nationalism is an attempt to transcend the undesirable relationship by a process of reflection, which creates a different constellation of symbols and assumptions. Moreover, Black Nationalism is an ideological movement of social, psychological and political portent[26] and is energized when:

1. there is a general expansion within the capitalist economy with blacks lagging behind;
2. the major white parties repudiate measures to address inequalities;
3. there is a rise of racist violence against black people;
4. the traditional black leadership is either unwilling or unable to articulate the grievances of the disaffected; and
5. the dominant discourse justifies the unequal division of power and resources in terms of black biological or cultural inferiority.[27]

The above chapter sets out the theoretical framework for this study and defines the subject matter of Pan-Africanism/Black Nationalism within the African Diaspora. The following chapter will examine the activities of the UNIA and the WMA the major Pan-African organizations that existed in Barbados in the post 1918 period.

2
The UNIA and the WMA

The UNIA

The year 1919 was a year of intense ferment throughout global Africa. Marcus Garvey and his UNIA movements were largely responsible for this development. In keeping with the global spread of Garveyism the first branch of the Barbadian UNIA was formed in 1919, largely through the efforts of John Beckles and Israel Lovell. The objectives of this organization were:

1. to teach Negroes to respect themselves, and join the organization, so that they might be able to win back the glories of Ethiopia;
2. to bring about the unity of Negroes;
3. to assist and advise them how to obtain the best wage possible for their labor;
4. to keep them out of the law courts, where they part with much of their hard-earned wages;
5. to collect money for the Black Star Line and their shops, stores and kindred objects.[1]

According to Tony Martin there were four UNIA branches located in Barbados: Westbury Road and Baxter's Road, St. Michael, Crab Hill, St. Lucy and Indian Ground, St. Peter.[2] However the local UNIA expert David Brown discovered that there were two additional branches, one in Half Moon Fort, St.

Lucy and the other in Venture, St. John.[3] It is important to note
that Gladstone Leacock the Garveyite leader from the Crab Hill
branch was a member of the UNIA in Cuba and on his return
to Barbados started the movement in rural Barbados. The UNIA
platform was largely concentrated on teaching the virtues of black
solidarity, black history and Pan-Africanism. The local Garveyites
recognized that black unity was an imperative in the quest to
transform their wretched, degraded conditions. Israel Lovell in
an address entitled "A Race for a Continent and a Continent for a
Race" stated that:

> . . . the UNIA is started for the purpose of teaching the
> Negroes how to respect themselves. . . . Every intelligent
> Negro should join the organization of the UNIA, so that
> they might win back the glories of Ethiopia. It is customary
> in this island to give the Negroes a few dollars and a pat on
> the shoulder and tell him he is well paid. . . . It is time that
> every Negro should rise to a sense of his condition.[4]

It must be noted that for centuries many Europeans referred
to Ethiopia as being synonymous with the continent of Africa
and not the country of Abyssinia that now bears this title. Many
Africans worldwide got some hope and inspiration from the
Biblical references to Ethiopia especially Psalms 68: 31 Princes
shall come out of Egypt, and Ethiopia shall stretch forth her hand
to mean that Africa's redemption was near. The Barbadian UNIA
like their counterparts elsewhere felt that this prophecy was about
to be fulfilled. This was very evident in the UNIA catechism:

> Q. What prediction made in the 68th Psalm and the 31st
> verse is now being fulfilled?
> A. Princes shall come out of Egypt; Ethiopia shall soon
> stretch out her hands unto God.
> Q. What does this prove?
> A. That Black Men will set up their own government in
> Africa, with rulers of their own race.[5]

Mr. F. Gittens a member of the UNIA felt the fulfilment of the prediction was around the corner, and he made the appeal for more Barbadians to get involved in the movement:

> The time has come that the Ethiopian has stretched out her hand unto God and he will help her. It is true that the Negroes have been hampered for a long time. The people in other parts of the world have been united together, and we in Barbados can be united also. Some people stand aside and look on. Others said, we will see what will happen, but that is not the way. We have all suffered together, and if we are liberated, we must be liberated together.[6]

Reverend Craigwell, another Garveyite, paid homage to Garvey for making the oppressed Africans feel a sense of nationhood by giving the UNIA a flag and all the other trappings of nationhood. He also demonstrated his knowledge of his African history and the present condition of the black race. He stated:

> Mr. Marcus Garvey has brought us a flag and a race. God is no respecter of persons. God gave us Africa. Our forefathers were stolen and brought out as slaves and our good land Africa was stolen from us. The cry of the oppressed of Barbados has gone up to God, and he has sent us Mr. Marcus Garvey, who has raised the Black Star Line. There is a hand outstretched across the waters, our destiny lies in our hands. There is justice and equality pending, but unless we are united we never will achieve it.[7]

Melvin Innis shows how serious the UNIA members were on the question of discipline:

> . . . his heart went out with grief for the downtrodden race. We are glad that we have joined hands with Marcus Garvey who is today at Liberty Hall, New York, holding a conference trying to reclaim what was stolen...We have

been oppressed but have been taught how to bear our oppression. Very often our people oppress us more than the white man. It is said that in the sweat of man's brow he should eat bread. We sweat, but we do not get what we sweat for. I exhort you to be loyal and law abiding. Any man who is tried and punished before a Judge or Magistrate will also be punished by the organization.[8]

Alexandria Gibbs, the lady president of the UNIA, addressing a gathering spoke to the issue as why there was a dwindling in the membership of the Garveyites and exhorted the African masses to see what was happening throughout the world as the various races were uniting in order to make themselves strong/stronger. She stated:

False teachers and preachers are responsible for our scantiness tonight, but in due season we will again Come together, only let us look upward and onward. We have lived to see our leader set free. Friends, organize yourself, it is for our good, let us bind ourselves together and form one mass formation, for only the fittest will survive. Look around and see what is happening. The yellow men are getting together, the whites are gathering together. So let us blacks also get together.[9]

Melvin Innis stated 'that every Negro is living in Hell." "He who is not living in hell is living next door to hell."[10] However, the members of the UNIA believed that if the black masses unite they could overcome all obstacles and redress the disabilities they were facing. "Let us unite so as to avoid insults and wrongdoing which we now suffer."[11]

The Garveyites preached the need for black people to unite so that they would be able to address the wretched conditions of the race. They also felt that the blackman/woman's first duty toward his/her race was the achievement of racial unity. Indeed, they believed that the UNIA was the only organization capable of solving the problems of the black man/woman. Tony Martin makes the point that by the 1920s, the UNIA became the virtual representative of the black population.[12] This occurred in an era when the majority of Blacks were denied the franchise because they could not meet the financial and property requirements to participate in the electoral process. John Alleyne, a former president of the UNIA Baxters Road branch, asserted that "the UNIA is the only association by which you solve the problem of the black man."[11] John Catwell predicted that "starvation is ahead of us, so the sooner you joined the UNIA the better, as you are bound to join us some day for the UNIA is the Negro only hope."[13]

The UNIA engaged in a form of embryonic trade unionism by seeking to organize the workers to ask for better pay and working conditions in an age where trade unions were outlawed. It was generally felt that the UNIA was fuelling the industrial ferment throughout the island, as was the case in Trinidad.

There have been a few small strikes within recent months each time confined to one class of workman, e.g. ship's carpenters, lighter men, and porters, and although individual members of the UNIA. have been known to advise these strikers, there is no evidence of the Association as a whole taking an active part. These strikes have always ended without trouble, the men behaving well during the strike and usually get an increase of wages, when they resume work.[14]

Additionally, the UNIA branches performed the functions of a mutual aid society.

The UNIA, in the tradition of the early Pan-Africanists, held a very strong emigrationist strand and African consciousness in their philosophy. Like many of their counterparts in America and other areas of the Diaspora many black people suffered from what Du Bois called the "double consciousness," while they lived outside of Africa and held legal citizenship in their respective countries they still saw themselves as Africans in exile. Tony Martin is of the view that the remembrance of Africa has dominated our being and our existence. We have never forgotten Africa and yet, at the same time, the powers that be have never felt comfortable with this remembrance.[15] The humiliation of the colonization of Africa was still fresh in the minds of the Garveyites. It must be noted that Ethiopia was an important symbol to Pan-Africanism. African evangelist had preached Ethiopianism (the gospel of worldwide African redemption) for over two centuries. Many of the preachers interpreted Psalms 68:31 " to mean that Africa's past glories shall be restored to Africa.[16] Ethiopianism in addition to being a religious dogma was also a trans- Atlantic political and literary movement. Ethiopianism was based on the idea that the ascendancy of the Europeans was only temporary, and that the divine providence of history was working to elevate the African peoples.

Moreover, Ethiopia's victory over the Italians at Adowa in 1896 further concretised the significance of Ethiopia. This victory inspired and gave black people worldwide new hope in the battle against expanding white domination. Asante stated:

> After the victory over Italy in 1896, Ethiopia acquired a special importance in the eyes of the Africans as the only surviving African State. After Adowa, Ethiopia became emblematic of African valour and resistance, the bastion of prestige and hope to thousands of Africans who were experiencing the full shock of European conquest and were beginning to search for an answer to the myth of African inferiority.[17]

The anthem of Garvey's UNIA was ode to Ethiopia, and one of the highest awards the UNIA bestowed was the distinguished order of Ethiopia. Therefore, Ethiopia/Africa was uppermost in the minds of the UNIA members.

Samuel Radway gives an example of the strong emigrationist

strand that was prevalent in the philosophy of the Garveyities, this was also evident in many of the slaves who yearned to return to Africa. He asserted:

> We should be proud to go back to Africa our forefathers' land; we are in a far distant land distributed throughout the West Indies. I don't hear my people saying that they are going to Africa, but to other places. You may say that you can't get to Africa, but if you do nothing and sit down God will not help you. Africa is not coming to you. . . . The pendulum of the Negroes clock is moving to and fro, and the time is not far off when the clock shall strike twelve for the Negroes of the world. . . . When I shall trod the soil of Africa, then I will say Lord now let thy servant depart in peace for my eyes have seen thy salvation.[18]

John Catwell like Garvey recognised that only Africans with skills/human capital could play an instrumental role in constructing the Great African Empire that would act as the custodian of African peoples everywhere and bring about the liberation of the race.

> We the children of the honourable Marcus Garvey must be up and doing if not we will be cast into oblivion. I want you all to be properly trained so that when you reach Africa you will be prepared. I have been to Africa three times. The honourable Marcus Garvey is coming to the island as a thief in the night to take those away to Africa.[19]

John Catwell Junior said:

> Africa is looking for every man to do his duty. The Hon. Marcus Garvey is one of the greatest men that ever lived; God has sent the Hon. Marcus Garvey as a leader of the Negroes. If the Negroes leave this island and go back to Africa, what will the island do? Lots of people are saying

the world is coming to an end, but it is not the world that is coming to an end, it is only the oppression of the Negro which is coming to an end.[20]

Melvin Innis, the UNIA President, urged his followers:

We are going forward fighting for Africa's redemption, don't be disheartened; don't believe that we are good for nothing. We are a working unit. I have read that our leader is again at liberty. Well we are glad for that, for we are supposed to see him, some day set at liberty, so don't lose faith, let us continue the fight. . . . Friends if we followed the dictates of Marcus Garvey, we are sure to achieve the object for which we aim. Africa is our aim and objective. It was the home of our ancestors, and we have got to redeem it. So let us work and work until we set our feet on its soil.[21]

Rupert Lewis is of the view that Garveyism was the most militant expression of the anti-colonial, anti-imperialist struggle of African peoples up to this period. The movement's official position as seen in this organizational document for UNIA leaders stated:

The culmination of all efforts of the UNIA must end in a Negro independent nation on the continent of Africa. This is to say everything must be contributed toward the final objective of having a powerful Nation for the Negro race. Negro nationalism is necessary. It is political power . . . and control.[22]

The UNIA gave the black masses a new, positive, conception of themselves, by seeking to emphasize black pride. Many of the Garveyites sought to challenge the falsehoods and distortions being propagated about Africans. They mentioned, "we are equal to any other man, we are not from the devil in hell, and they (referring to the white man) are not from Heaven."[23] John Alleyne argued "we have the same five senses as the other races and why not let us put them to the test."[24] Melvin Innis proudly proclaimed:

I was never ashamed of being a Negro; I am proud because I am a Negro. There are thousand of Negroes who are ashamed because they are Negroes, but the time is coming when the whites will wish they were black.[25]

The authorities in Barbados, like those through out the Caribbean were very concerned with the activities of the UNIA. They were particularly concerned with the contents of the *Negro World*, the mouthpiece of Garvey's movement. In fact the *Negro World* was blamed for causing disturbances in Belize, Trinidad, the United States and Central America. Therefore, the reactionary regimes in the Caribbean sought to curb the introduction of this paper. The Governor of Barbados argued that the introduction of such legislation would only stir up trouble without any chance of becoming law. Moreover, the Governor believed that the UNIA would die a natural death. The Solicitor General, who incidentally was black, felt that "the *Negro World* performed a useful service, it was good for the Barbadian coloured man to see the disabilities of the Negro in America as he should be better contented with his position here." The Central Intelligence Department argued that the object of the *Negro World* seemed to be to stir up trouble amongst the black races of the world. However, the Barbadian government did introduce a Seditious Publications Ordinance in 1920.[26]

The Governor seemed to be very scared of the UNIA, this was evident in his response as to whether the UNIA should be the official diplomatic body representing British West Indian Workers in Cuba. The Governor vehemently objected to this suggestion. He argued that the "UNIA was too dangerous in Barbados, and if it was recognized in Cuba this would increase its stature in Barbados and lead to problems for 'British Imperialism'."

If the Cuban branch was recognized as the centre of protection of the interest of the British West Indians in that country, I foresee that the society would obtain a status in this country that might be very inconvenient. It would certainly result in a very large membership, and the hotheads in the Association would be awakened to renewed zeal to stir up trouble between the two races.[27]

The Governor mentioned that there were two UNIA branches in Bridgetown. One was composed of more solid men, who lacked any distinctly anti- white proclivities. But he said that the other branch was disloyal. In fact, the Governor stated that some members of the UNIA had been burning canes in recent times and were becoming very restive.[28]

From the inception of the UNIA the police were closely monitoring their meetings. The Governor indicated that the UNIA had sent threatening letters to the planters and were encouraging the workers to strike. It was strongly felt that the UNIA members were actively involved in the industrial ferment that was taking place in the country. The Governor, in response to these developments, held a meeting with the leading planters advising them to pay their workers a decent wage to spare Barbados the scourge of insurrection that was taking place in the neighbouring Caribbean territories.[29]

It is easy to say that no trouble can come to Barbados, if you are satisfied that the laboring class are as well off now as under the pre-war conditions despite he . . . increased cost of living, you have no reason to fear criticism. If on the other hand laborers cannot earn a sufficiency to maintain their families and themselves throughout the year surely it is advisable to put the matter on a sound business footing. You have had good years for your industry and it is not surprising that the labouring classes here as elsewhere should desire to benefit by the better times.[30]

The police authorities were quite fearful that Marcus Garvey might pass through Barbados. Rumours were rife that Garvey was coming to Barbados and the UNIA and the Working Men's Association members were expecting Marcus Garvey in Barbados on the 4th of April 1928. As a form of respect and homage none of the members of these Pan-African organizations plan to work, all of them were going to see 'Marcus Garvey the originator of the red, black and green' — the leader that they held in great awe and veneration. While the police intelligence had not discovered whether Marcus Garvey was coming to Barbados, they suggested that it would not be advisable for Garvey to come to the island. Moreover, they suggested that Garvey should be informed through the Jamaican government that should he come to Barbados he would not be allowed to land.[31] It was strongly felt that the Expulsion of Undesirables Act of March 1927 was passed after the authorities heard that Garvey was planning to visit Barbados. Section 8 states:

> If it appears to the Governor that it is expedient for the preservation of the peace and good order of the Island that any person coming within section two of this Act who the Governor has reason had reason to believe is about to arrive or may arrive in the island should be prohibited from landing in the Island, the Governor may, if he thinks fit, make an expulsion order against such person. No person against whom such an order has been made shall be permitted to land in the Island, and if, after service upon him of such order, any person does so land, he may be arrested and deported from the Island in such a manner as the Governor may direct, and pending his deportation he may be detained in custody.[32]

Tony Martin mentions that Marcus Garvey stopped in transit in Barbados on November 15, 1928 but did not land. However, Garvey visited Barbados in 1937 where he spoke to a mammoth crowd at the Queen's Park steel shed.[33]

It is important to note that many females played important roles in the movement. It must be mentioned that the UNIA was structured like many African American churches, with a male president and other male officers along with a female president and female officers; whose task was to look after the female auxiliaries and juvenile divisions. Alexandria Gibbs served as a lady president, Anne Hooper was a lady president and Dorcas Bennett served as a lady vice president. These women also played an integral role in educating many children in their night schools. In addition they were instrumental in distributing the *Negro World* and other progressive literature.

With the imprisonment of Marcus Garvey between 1925-1930, the UNIA branches worldwide suffered some major decline. The Barbadian UNIA like the other branches worldwide saw a dwindling of its membership. The local movement suffered from internal and leadership squabbles; a shortage of funding, adverse propaganda which resulted in the reduction of its membership; and many of the middle class Blacks left the organization to be part of the Democratic League, since they felt that the Democratic League would present the best opportunity to facilitate their agenda.

The WMA

In 1924, Dr. Charles Duncan O'Neal, Clennel Wickham and some other progressive minded individuals started a political party called the Democratic League. According to Marvin Will, the Democratic League was formed largely due to the motivation of Marcus Garvey and was the most important political group to come on the Barbadian scene before the 1937 crisis.[34] O'Neal was strongly influenced by Garvey and began to organize the black working class, along similar lines as Garvey, with a "clear viable political agenda."[35] The Democratic League was the first political party to emerge in Barbados. It was primarily a liberal middle class grouping that sought to promote socialism and political activism. Several Garveyites immediately threw their support behind the Democratic League.

The Workingmen's Association, the industrial wing of the Democratic League, was founded in 1926. O' Neal recognised the need for an organization to further the economic objectives of the working class, to represent them in their labour market, and to assist workers to invest their accumulated savings for their collective good. The WMA functioned as the industrial and business arm of the Democratic League. This organization was comprised mainly of artisans. The WMA had two offices that were located in Bridgetown, one at the corner of Baxter's Road and one in Reed Street. The main planks of the WMA platform were compulsory education, manhood suffrage, unemployment allowance, workingmen's compensation and old age pensions. Moses Small, one of the main figures of the WMA, stated, "we are clamouring for compulsory education and old age pension, otherwise you will be spending your future life at the old almshouse."[36] However, the WMA placed tremendous emphasis on black unity, black self-help and power, and the need for organization.

Moses Small, Moses Taitt, Edwin Turpin and George Belle, were the leading spokesmen of the WMA and they consistently argued that the major task for the recovery of black people culturally and politically must begin with the recapture of Ethiopia as the Mecca for the continent.[37] Moses Small stated:

> We (the black race) will not be satisfied until we walk on the continent of Africa, then we will sing 'lustily.' We are clamouring for better conditions for our people. We are scattered all over the world and not represented. The time will come when God said that we will rebuild the temple.[38]

Like the UNIA, the WMA concentrated heavily on preaching the gospel of organization. Moreover, the WMA was very mindful of being infiltrated by operatives of the Special branch; it is not known how successful they were or what they did to prevent this. George Belle stated:

We are united here together for a just cause. . . . This movement you all heard about and know needs good manage-
ment? Many movements were organized in Barbados by
other people and all are gone to the dogs. If anything goes
wrong, come forward as a man and let us hear what you
have to say instead of telling outsiders, but as long as we
allow this worthless policy to remain into our breast, this
movement will surely go to the ground and the white man
will laugh.

Some men have been promised $200 to go into the or-
ganization . . . that they will be able to destroy this movement, that is how Garvey was destroyed because he had
black men on his side who went forward and told the Government all this that was being said.[39]

The WMA, holding true to its socialist conviction sought to critique the political economy of Barbados by explaining to its con-
stituents what was a capitalist; and examined the superstructure
of Barbadian society by explaining the role of the Police force. It
is very important to note that the WMA sang the anthem of the
UNIA:

Ethiopia, thou land of our fathers,
Thou land where the Gods love to be
As storm clouds at night suddenly gather
Our armies come rushing to thee.
We must in the fight be victorious
When swords are thrust outward to gleam;
For us will the vict'ry be glorious
When led by the red the black and the green.
Chorus:
Advance, advance to victory
Let Africa be free;
Advance to meet the foe
With the might of the red, black and green.[40]
Horace Campbell posits the view that the anthem of the UNIA

was a call for military preparations in anticipation of the inevitable struggle for black liberation.[41]

The WMA also sang the hymn of the Red Flag at all of their meetings. Tony Martin argues that the bodies of thought represented by Garvey and the communists were deceptively similar. Both were anti-capitalist and anti-imperialist, both sought to organize around the masses.[42] George Belle goes even further by stating that the programme of a Marxist at that time was the programme of Garvey; it was anti-colonial and anti-imperialist.[43] In Barbados Clennel Wickham used the pages of the Herald to propagate the gospel of Marxism. In addition, the *Negro Worker* edited by George Padmore was being circulated, Geiss argues that the *Negro Worker* fulfilled a Pan-African as well as a communist function.[44] In addition the *West Indian Organiser* was also being read. When one examines the rhetoric of the Pan-Africanists it is clear that they were influence by the ideas emanating from the *Organizer*.

Today the majority of working people are slowly dying from undernourishment; the black children who are to be the men of tomorrow are all rickety from want and milk. Unemployment is corroding the fibre of thousands of city workers who daily hang around the city squares. The workers on the plantations slave for the starvation wage of twenty-four cents a day. Their children are forced to work under the broiling sun for six cents a day. Brothers! Why do we, 90% of the population, who do all the work in the Islands permit a handful of white aristocrats to subject us to these miseries? It is because we submit to the low wage policy, the Pie in the sky and hell fire doctrines of the lying robber employers. Only through organized struggle for some of the product of our toil can we accomplish this. Praying to God will not help us. We have been doing this all along and have constantly become poorer, while the idle rich have fattened on our blood. Last year we produced 110,000 tons of sugar alone. This sugar was sold by the Employers for $4,400,000. The bulk of it went into the bankrolls of the Yearwoods, Piles and other parasites who infest our verdant islands with their idle and lordly presence. This is the root cause of our sufferings. Shall we continue in these conditions of slavery, or will we organize and fight?[45]

Moses Small provides an excellent analysis of the superstructure of the Barbarbadian political economy:

The labour movement said we are not satisfied with the flesh and the blood we give for labour? We want as much by which we can live by. . . . What do you understand by capitalist? This is the man who made laws for you to obey and protect themselves from the labouring men. The police force comes between to protect the capitalist from the labouring man. This money, which builds the capitalist, is from the fruit of unpaid labourers.[46]

The WMA was involved in raising the consciousness of workers to fight against the Better Security Bill; they interpreted this Bill as an attempt to re-enslave the citizens of the island. The notion of slavery/re-enslavement was very sensitive to the WMA and the UNIA; in their meetings slavery was always discussed in order to explain the condition of Blacks in Barbados, and the condition of Global Africans. Therefore it is understandable that the WMA would resist any perceived covert attempts to re-enslave them. The WMA kept many meetings and sought to mobilize workers throughout the island to fight against this piece of legislation.

Workingmen and Women Wake Up!
Come to Reed Street Hall
And sign the petition to the Secretary of State for the colonies
And Let Us Kill the "Back to Slavery" Law recently made by the lawmakers—
It is now or never, your Liberty is at Stake:

The Wolf is at the door. "British Subjects never shall be slaves."[47]

Edwin Turpin and William Marshall, two members of the WMA, visited the rural parishes of St. Peter and St. Lucy and sought to mobilize the workers to sign a petition against the Better Security Bill. Indeed, the battle against the Better Security Bill saw the WMA engaged in probably their most significant struggle. The WMA kept a series of meetings throughout the city and its environs to inform the masses of labouring people about the Better Security Bill. Turpin and Marshall were of the view that the people in the country/rural districts had responded better that those in the Bridgetown and its environs and wanted to do everything in their power to fight against this offensive bill. While this might well have been the case this comparison seemed like a challenge for workers in the city to respond with a little more gusto.

George Belle stated:

That the lawyer has criticised this bill, and said it is dangerous . . . it affects all the poor working classes. The Attorney General introduced this bill, which was hastily drawn up… This was taken from the English act of 1875, which gives the police and the magistrate illegal powers.[48]

This Bill so infuriated the WMA. that one witnessed a militancy that was not present before. Cyprian Robinson stated:

I am a full-blooded Negro; I am a member of the ILP. This Bill is a serious one, which tends to enslave the sons of free men… I am not afraid to die, my hands have killed many white men, I was in the British Navy, we are not going to fight not yet, but we don't know when. We refuse to stop these meetings and when we get much stronger we will put then near the Public Buildings. We are not teaching race hatred we are teaching our people to better their condition, all the doors of the outside world are closed against us, before people could go from Barbados to America by the thousands and now only five persons a month.[49]

It is not clear whether Robinson fought in the British Navy but the Better Security Bill made him extremely angry. However, Robinson has his hands on the pulse by linking the Better Securities Bill with developments in Panama and elsewhere. From about 1905-1914 about some twenty thousand Barbadians went to Panama to work on the construction of the canal. Barbadians had also emigrated to the United States and to several countries throughout the West Indies. Historically emigration provided an outlet to the energies of the people, much like a safety valve but now this avenue seemed to be closing. The tone of Robinson's rhetoric is one of acute militancy in the vein of the African Blood Brotherhood who fought pitched battles with white mobs in Oklahoma.

On another occasion Cyprian Robinson demanded:

We want the capitalists to understand that we are learning to love each other and we want them to give us a little that we can live on. We are teaching socialism, what we want is the gods of Barbados to give us a living wage to both men and women, if we were to teach hatred the intelligent section of the criminal department would know where we are. Because this association is in its infancy they want to frighten you away, but if you stick together, it will show love, if we were much stronger the men at the intelligence Department will leave us. You must continue with the Association and in the 1930s when we come together in one sealed body our great force will be unstoppable, . . . we will then be true Negroes.[50]

The WMA and the UNIA worked very closely together during the late twenties and early thirties. Indeed, many of the WMA members had been UNIA members or were still Garveyites. The WMA and the UNIA held a demonstration on the 7th of August 1933, to commemorate the centenary of William Wilberforce, for his role in the abolition of slavery and they also paid tribute to Booker T. Washington, Frederick Douglas and Marcus Garvey. The procession travelled from the Workers Hall, and travelled along Baxter's Road, Tudor Street, Milk Market, Broad Street, Trafalgar Square, Constitution and Belmont Road and stopped near Government House where they played the anthem and continued by way of Welches, Bridge Road, Hindsbury Road, Bank Hall, and Eagle Hall and back to the Workers Hall.[51]

The WMA consistently paid homage to Marcus Garvey. Moses Small stated:

> Friends and comrades, this meeting tonight is for the purpose of the commemoration of Marcus Garvey, our great leader, the greatest Negro that ever lived. He is the mouthpiece of God, after having served honourably among us for a short time he was placed in prison because he taught race salvation of the labouring poor. This is the third year since he was in prison, during which time his health is very much impaired, he has petitioned the United States authority and asked that he may be released but they took no notice of him. Marcus Garvey has done no wrong to any one; he was only leading his people that a better nation may be rise than the one at present. Two thousand years ago Christ was preaching the gospel of God to the people for this reason he was crucified so it is with Marcus Garvey but they placed him in prison, he has paid the penalty for the Negro race.[52]

On another occasion Moses Small said:

> The 19th chapter of Isaiah spoke of him; Egypt means black and that nation cried unto the Lord and he promised that he will send them a saviour and we believe that the Lord sent Garvey to us and if that be so we shall be delivered.[53]

Edwin Turpin in his address stated:

. . . Marcus Garvey is the greatest Negro in the world…he has promoted human progress. The time has come that you should unite together, today what we are doing is from the doctrine of Marcus Garvey, he has done no wrong, he only brought the Negro to light and if we follow his teachings the time will come when we shall take our hats off for Marcus Garvey. He is placed in prison for the redemption of Africa, those fellas got together and said that he is teaching nation-hood and Africa will be redeemed, . . . if we allow him to continue, let us put him in prison and they did. . . . He have voiced the redemption of Africa. . . . I will continue to preach this gospel of Garvey. Any man who fails to preach this gospel will never get any further. . . . We have now in our midst a great association which has sprung from the gospel of Garvey. We are equal to any other men; we are not from the devil in Hell, they are not from heaven, and if you come together you cannot fail. If all the Negroes had raise their voices to protest against what was done to Garvey they would release him. The other nations have got together to fight against our father land, the African fought well but owing to might certain portions of land were taken and divided up between the other nations but the time will come when it will be redeemed that we may be able to enjoy some of the blessings of our father land.[54]

David Brown argues that the theology of the African Orthodox Church was very evident at the prayer meetings held by the UNIA and the WMA activists. These Pan-Africanists sought to interpret the scriptures from a Black Nationalist perspective. Black people were said to be the Israelites, and their suffering was likened to the biblical Israelites, the chosen people of God. Indeed, many of the early Pan-Africanists strongly believed that the "cross preceded the crown," that suffering was a necessity before the victory. The teachings of the established churches, especially the Anglican and the Catholic were attacked. These churches were accused of being 'deceivers and shy pirates', who pointed the masses towards the sky while they were living like dogs on earth. Black Barbadians were taught to embrace aspects of Christianity, which portrayed the black race in a positive light.[55] Garvey had stated:

> The Negro is now accepting the religion of the real Christ, not the property-robbing, gold-stealing, diamond-exploiting Christ, but the Christ of Love, Justice and Mercy. The Negro wants no more of the white man's religion as it applies to his race, for it is a lie and a farce; it is propaganda pure and simple to make fools of a race and rob the precious world, the gift of God to man, and to make it the exclusive home of pleasure, prosperity and happiness for those who have enough intelligence to realize that God made them masters of their fate and architects of their own destinies.[56]

The Italian-Abyssinia War, which witnessed the concretization of the bonds of Pan-Africanism, breathed new life into the WMA and the UNIA. These Pan-African organizations, like their compatriots throughout Global Africa, rallied to Ethiopia's cause, by keeping prayer vigils and holding fund raising activities on the benefit of the Ethiopian people. Wickham, writing in the Advocate Weekly stated:

> The interest shown by West Indian Communities in the Italo-Abyssinian quarrel is significant. In every colony, big and small, there have been public meetings and demonstrations, and strongly worded resolutions have been dispatched to his Majesty's Government.[57]

Horace Campbell is of the view "that black workers in the Caribbean were in the forefront of the opposition to the Italian invasion of Abyssinia." According to him "many blacks declared that they should be allowed to fight on the side of their brothers and sisters in Ethiopia."[58] For example, in St. Lucia the international Friends of Ethiopia denounced the Foreign Enlistment Act and passed the following resolution:

> In view of the provoked aggression of Italy against unarmed Ethiopia, the penal clause of the above act be waived in so far as it applies to West Indians, to permit St. Lucians who may desire to do so volunteering to go to Ethiopia.[59]

According to Campbell, similar resolutions were passed in Dominica, Barbados, Jamaica, Trinidad and Antigua.

Moreover David Brown asserted that the intensity of the local UNIA and WMA's protest against Italy was so acute that it became difficult for the colonial authorities to ignore the feelings of the black population on any racial or political issue. Indeed the Governor ordered an investigation in Barbados for the presence of any Italian missionaries, who if found were to be deported. This directive was viewed as a method to appease local tempers while seeking revenge for the British missionaries that were expelled from Ethiopia.[60]

The colonialists in the Caribbean warned the colonialists in Africa to expect similar protestations:

> In certain West Indian dependencies a very considerable degree of interest, amounting at times to undesirable excitement, has been invoked among the local population by the Italian Abyssinia war. . . . While I have no doubt that, at any rate among the more advanced sections of native opinion in certain African dependencies, the present Italian Abyssinia war is followed with much interest, I have received no reports indicating that the war has aroused in any African dependency the same degree of excitement as it has in certain West Indian dependencies.[61]

William Scott captures the mood of the African world at this juncture, he states "members of the dark-skinned races readily identified with the plight of the Solomonic empire and sought to aid its cause in sundry ways, having linked the Ethiopian struggle with their own battles against racism and imperialism."[62] Du Bois the noted Pan-Africanist stated that Black and Brown people all over had been aroused as seldom before.[63] Makin stated:

> Most astonishing, the fervour with which Negroes all over the World had taken the Abyssinian war to heart. Negroes in the United States and the British possessions have not hesitated to declare themselves on the side of Africa's last empire. This fervour has led to riots in Harlem and to hysterical prayer meetings among Negroes in London.[64]

Many of the WMA members tempered their Pan-African activities and concentrated on electoral politics as they sought to get members of the Democratic League elected to sit in the House of Assembly. They believed that black politicians would be in a better position to articulate their fundamental concerns and implement policies to address their stark conditions. However, the Democratic League shifted to the politics of conservatism by concentrating on issues that affected the middle class instead of focusing on working class concerns. In addition, the death of Charles Duncan O'Neal and the removal of the socialist Clennel Wickham from the Barbadian landscape witnessed a mellowing of genuine working class concerns. Indeed, the UNIA and the WMA were now spent forces and lacked the energy and inspirational leadership to take them forward.

The UNIA and the WMA played a crucial role in building the foundations of 20th century Pan-Africanism in Barbados. These early Pan-Africanists fought against extreme odds as they sought to raise the consciousness of the black masses, in their quest for dignity, social justice, and economic and political advancement in a very hostile environment. Many of the pressing issues they agitated for were not realized because these individuals were visionaries who were many years ahead of their time. Nevertheless, the UNIA and the WMA provided the framework and several issues for subsequent Pan-Africanists to agitate for. The following chapter will examine how the Pan-Africanists built on the work of these Pan-Africanists and how they were catapulted into the leadership of the masses, the issues they discussed and how the repressive state apparatus cut them down.

3
The Pan-Africanists in 1937

In 1937, Clement Osborne Payne arrived in Barbados from the Garvey infected land of Trinidad (Trinidad contained 30 UNIA branches). He was a member of the Negro Welfare Cultural and Social Association in Trinidad, and this Garveyite organization worked in close collaboration with Tubal Uriah Butler and the Oil Field and Trade Workers.[1] Payne quickly enlisted the support of the veteran Pan-Africanists Israel Lovell and Fitzgerald Chase, and sought to mobilize the Barbadian masses to unite and build a strong workers organization. Payne described his mission "as one to assist in improving the method of living and procedure of organization in Barbados." He held about seventeen meetings in the area of Bridgetown, where he spoke about race relations in Barbados, black cultural suppression and the Italian invasion of Ethiopia. Payne's rallying cry at these meetings was "educate, agitate but don't violate."[2]

Payne wanted to organize the workers into a strong trade union force, in order to counter the power of the white corporate elite. He was cognisant that the only vehicle to counter capitalism was strong trade unionism. It must be mentioned that trade unions were outlawed at this juncture. Payne sought to move the discourse from the parochial Barbadian context and informed the masses of the industrial turmoil occurring throughout the West Indies. The coal workers of St. Lucia and the oil workers of Trinidad followed quickly on the heels of St. Kitts. According to Payne, this industrial ferment was a manifestation of the rising consciousness of the black West Indians. He attracted large crowds of workers whenever he spoke. Beckles is of the view that "Payne succeeded in combining the incisive socio-political analysis of Wickham with the organizational drive of O'Neal, and in a short period of time captured the imagination of the radicals and the younger generation."[3] He spoke about race relations in Barbados, black cultural suppression, the Pan-African nature of Garveyism, and the Italian invasion of Abyssinia. Ernest Mottley mentions that "Payne's politics were of the black versus white nature, and thought that his ideological position was unlike O'Neal's communistic." According to Beckles, "Mottley like many middle class blacks, considered political references by black radicals to African liberation and black cultural nationalism, as racist attacks upon the dominant Euro-cultural element within the colony." Therefore, persons of the black middle class considered "Garveyities racist, and Payne's criticism of the liberal black middle class communistic."[4]

The white ruling class in Barbados felt very uncomfortable with the message emanating from Payne's platform; therefore they looked for a way to stop him. Payne was placed under heavy police surveillance. Payne, who was born in Trinidad, of Barbadian parentage and brought to Barbados when he was four years, was arrested on the charge that he made a false declaration of his place of birth when he arrived in the island. However, this development did not satisfy his followers, who viewed this as an attempt to silence Payne, because he had opened the eyes of the masses to many disabilities they were currently facing.

Massive crowds followed Clement Payne to and from his trial; he was convicted and fined £10. Payne appealed the fine and wanted to lead a march to the Governor's house to publicly appeal the decision before the Governor and protest against this miscarriage of justice. However, the police refused to give him permission and Payne kept his last meeting in Golden Square where he stated:

People of Bridgetown, friends and enemies, we are here again with the object of organizing you, but before I start to talk about organization, I will tell you my trouble with the Constabulary. . . . I am charged with landing improperly and for giving a false statement relative to my place of birth. . .

I have come to the slums to organize you, because Mr. Ramsey McDonald organised the people of the slums of England. I could have gone among the aristocrats but they are deceitful. . . . The Police Department has started a War against me, the detectives follow me daily and even if I go to take out a lady friend the detectives are there also. I want all of you, who are not working to come out on Thursday morning and hear my case, for I am a sworn enemy of oppression. I am harassed by Major Goddard, Plunkett and the detective sergeant. I have not plotted to blow up any district; I am in sympathy with some of the Police, because they have to do what they are told, so as to get bread and butter. I respect the office of the Chief of Police but not him personally. I have been shadowed and suffered intolerance from the police department, I am not a fascist, Communist or Bolshevist. . . If the Government succeeds in deporting me, wherever I may be my words must be with you, 'Crying out for British Justice' for my people. Trinidad, British Guiana and St. Vincent are all organised; what of Barbados who boast of Harrison College and Combermere School etc. Is Barbados going to stand up and allow St. Vincent, with thirty two thousand people show the way? It's a shame and disgrace to Barbados. The Central Foundry strike was not published in Barbados, yet the *Advocate Newspaper* published the Trinidad strike. Why the hell did they not publish the Barbadian strike? I am saying boycott the *Advocate Newspaper* it's no good.

. . . The aristocrats and middle-class people of Barbados need no organization, it's only you the poor labourers; who if you get hurt on the job get nothing, and that is why you should have Old Age Pension, Workmen's Compensation and Compulsory Education. . . . The day of Uncle Tom

Negroes is dead. I am a man of action; your elementary schools in this Island are always teaching children about great white men nothing is taught about the great black Poets, Scientists, Philosophers etc. They should be taught about the black literature. They are taught about Dickens etc., not Dickens the Police; Charles Dickens. They should be told about Marryshow and C.W. Wickham. England and France sold out the Ethiopians to the Italians. It is the intention of the other race to annihilate us. It is an advantage that has been taken of the Ethiopians and you should tell your children about these cursed things.[5]

Payne, while demonstrating his unity in the struggle with all oppressed black people, strongly echoed the sentiments of Marcus Garvey who asserted that:

The time has come for the Blackman to forget and cast behind him his hero worship and adoration of other races, and to start out immediately to create and emulate heroes of his own. We must canonize our own saints, create our own martyrs, and elevate to positions of fame and honour Black men and women who have made their distinct contributions to our racial history.[6]

Therefore, Payne wanted the black masses to be taught about their great and wonderful history. He also wanted the schools to desist from teaching Euro-centric literature and history. From the days of Blyden all the great theoreticians of Pan-Africanism/Black Nationalism have always stressed the need for the study of black history. Payne continued to launch his attack on all of those institutions he believed were responsible for the wretched plight of the black masses on the island.

The Chamber of Commerce and provision Dealers are all organized. Organise for the sake of your children. The fore-parents of Governor Young and Fletcher and the Chief of Police Dickens thought that their sons would one-day come out to rule us, as they have paved the way for their children, let us do the same for ours. You black women must stand shoulder to shoulder with the men and assist in building the character of your children and don't grumble. I am a member of the British Commonwealth of Nations and I am saying that Uncle Tom days are dead. It is a fact that some of us suffer from an inferiority complex. I want you people to talk to the white man just as I talk to the Colonial Secretary, Commander Wynne and Colonel Dickens. The Goodmans mystery case and the James Street Murder case were not solved. Why the chief of Police do not use his Scotland Yard methods in tracing them instead of hunting innocent men like Chase and me.

In this Island they have third gangs and cricket-gangs working for nothing, those are matters that need attention. Religion is retarding the progress of the West Indian Negro.

In 1914, Russia was a backward nation, today she is impregnable. She has dug down all the churches with their £1,000 bells and builds ammunition factories. Every black man should have hate for religion especially Roman Catholic Religion. Pope Pius has 5,000 shares in the factories, which make poisonous gas. The Bishop of Trinidad went among the oil field people during the recent strike, but before that he did not have the guts to get in the pulpit and tell the capitalists that he is paying out starvation wages. Don't be fooled anymore by the religion dope. The white man's heaven is his V8 car, radios and four meals per day. You want the same. Religion is fooling you people, you black people must study economy and industry, and stop confessing to Roman Catholic Fathers, there is only one father. The others who call themselves fathers are hypocrites. It is they who have the world upside down. If you are to eat 4 meals a day, you must be organized. You must honour God, respect the laws of your country and love your brother. Boycott the Courts. Thursday will be a red-letter day, come down and hear my case, you must educate, agitate, concentrate but don't violate. Boycott the Advocate Newspaper. I am going to make this spot the Mecca of organization in this Island. Bad things have been said about Golden Square, but I have found my services better appreciated than elsewhere in this Island. I now ask for a substantial contribution to assist me.[7]

Payne launched a serious broadside against religion, this demonstrated his familiarity with the branch of European Marxism which saw religion as an opiate that prevented the masses from demanding what was rightly theirs because they believed that when they got to heaven they will get everything that was previously denied to them. Moreover, the Roman Catholic Church was singled out for special mention because of the stand the church took when the Italians invaded Abyssinia and massacred the people with their poison gas.

Menzies Chase at the same meeting stated:

Tonight is a serious night, and I am as serious as death, two days ago I was being shadowed, I am no criminal, neither is Mr. Payne a criminal, we have been suffering from inferiority complex. Payne is my friend, I am going to court and stand by him...I want you to be serious next Thursday morning and to turn out in your numbers, I am not a "Britisher," I am an "Alien." If Payne was not talking the truth, why would the police hunt him down? He is not telling some people to cut off other peoples hands or feet...If we were organized in this Country, proper inquiry would have been made in connection with the strike, it would have been placed before the representative of the House... and the men would certainly get more money. Barbadians are the most law-abiding Citizens in the world, they are contented with nothing. The little confusion in Barbados is caused through Marcus Garvey who is expected to pass through here, and it is believed that Payne would have a delegation to meet him, but we are out for organizing, a serious time is ahead. . . . We are also making arrangements to have an emancipation celebration on the 2nd of August 1937 and we are asking everybody to contribute wholeheartedly.[8]

Payne was subsequently arrested and deported from the island. In his absence, Israel Lovell, Menzies Chase, Darnley Alleyne and Ulric Grant sought to provide some leadership to the masses. Hilary Beckles stated "that with the removal of Payne during the trial, the UNIA had assumed temporary leadership of the workers movement."[9]

Israel Lovell, the veteran Pan-Africanist, reiterated the call by the UNIA, the WMA and by Clement Payne for the people to become organized. He said:

They can't deport me; they can only send me to jail. If you people had retaliated the town would still be smoking and some policemen would be in the cemetery...I know what is going to take place; I can die now. Payne was brutalised this morning, but don't be afraid of what is happening. Let us organize and withstand violence. If we were organized Goddard would have thought a thousand times before he touched Payne. There is no justice in Coleridge Street, for Judges sit down and misjudge us.[10]

At another meeting Lovell stated:

We cannot steal from the white man because if we take anything it will only be some of what they had stolen from our fore parents for the past 250 years but Christ has been crucified to day, Awake friends this is the beginning. Let all the Goddards know that we are not taking things as before and that we want bread and butter just like Bowring and

Darnley Dacosta. I am fighting this cause until death. The situation in Barbados is a funny one we make the wealth of this country and get nothing in return. Our slave fathers were in a better condition than we are today. The world is against us, so let us unite in mass formation and stand up like men. Instead of Payne being in jail it should be Goddard. If we were organized before Goddard handled Payne yesterday, he would have bitten off his fingernails. For even if he had six men of war in the Bay and all the policemen and volunteers with rifles he would not be saved, If this ever happen again don't run, for they don't have jail sufficient to hold all of us.[11]

The above speech by Lovell demonstrated his intimate knowledge and incisive critique of the economic and social relations between the workers and the economic ruling class. It also demonstrated the strong influence of an emerging black radicalism that was tied to socialism. In a meeting at Carrington Village where over 1400 people were in attendance Lovell stated:

We people cultivate the land and get nothing in return, the white man has it in his pockets and we are looking to heaven only; the white man has V8, radio, piano, turkey, ham and eggs and champagne. Clement Payne is a martyr; he has made history in the island of Barbados. He was leading a peaceful people to Government house to ask for milk and bread and the police authorities waylaid and arrested him. They are only12% white in this island against 88% of the masses so don't be afraid.[12]

Lovell was charged for sedition and imprisoned for five years thereby removing the principal Pan-African figure, who had been around from the inception of the UNIA, and who had the respect and support of the masses and would have been able to use this influence in building the first genuine mass Pan-African organization.

Ulric Grant, a Barbadian who had spent some time in the United States, seemed to be very familiar with the UNIA movement in the United States especially in Harlem, the unofficial capital of Garveyism. Grant stated:

. . . It is a shame and a disgrace to see the injustice, which was done. The administration of justice to day was done in a high-handed way, before Payne entered the courts he was convicted. Payne was only trying to educate his people politically and the capitalistic element has started a war against him. They have everything for themselves and yet are trying to exploit the poor masses. If we don't unite we will be found wanting. The magistrate fined Payne £10 for nothing. Barbados has the worst jails in the world. It is run on a slave basis. In other prisons you can read and smoke, Barbados jails was only made for the Negroes. Let us fight for the rights of ourselves and our children. We are mistreated. I fear no man on earth and as long as I have breath in my body I will expose the wrong doings in this Island.

If Unrest starts in Barbados the capitalistic element will be responsible for it. We will have to fight for all we want, but not with sticks except we have to. If we don't fight we will get nowhere for it is a shame and disgrace to know that slavery still exists in Barbados. Organization is essential to any people, so let us combine and get in mass formation. Marcus Garvey organized 400,000,000 people. The capitalistic element is doing their best to get Payne out of Barbados. Payne and I will die for you. Let us get together and march to government house and put our needs to the Governor.

The capitalists prey on anyone who tries to uplift the masses. One of these days the capitalists will wake up and find things in a drastic way. The decision in Payne's case has me inflamed. I rather die by the sword than by a famine. In Harlem people picketed a store because it did not employ black men and women. We can only do these things if we were organised.[13]

Grant sought to demonstrate to the people the power of organization by utilising the example of what he observed in Harlem. At another meeting at Golden Square Grant said:

Tonight is a serious night; we are here fighting a just cause. The capitalistic element has been trying long ago to get him out of the way. The white men are all for themselves and are depriving us of our bread and butter. The policemen of the Island are only protecting the capitalistic element and they have no sympathy for the masses. How long will we stand for such treatment? The masses are exploited and there is no one to fight on the behalf of the masses. The reason why the foundry strike failed was because the masses were not organized. Organization would capsize the capitalistic element that are exploiting the people. The merchants are the Capitalistic element that are oppressing us.[14]

The repressive state apparatus also imprisoned Ulric Grant and the other Pan-African leaders who had taken over the leadership of the labour movement. One must note that Grant was sentence to ten years imprisonment and Lovell and Alleyne were sentence to spend five years imprisonment. The police were said to have killed fourteen persons and wounding over forty-seven and arrested over four hundred in the disturbances that followed after Payne was deported. The imprisonment and repression prevented the Pan-Africanists from entrenching themselves as the leaders of the labour movement in the post-1937 period as many middle class individuals took centre stage and the Pan-Africanist movement disappeared from the centre of the labour struggles. Indeed, it was only with the Peoples Progressive Movement/Black Star in the 1960s that the Pan-African project got national attention again. The next Chapter will look at the activities of the PPM as they sought to transform the economic and political structure of Barbados.

4
The PPM/*Black Star*

The 1960s was a period of intense ferment and radicalisation throughout Africa, Asia, Latin America and the United States. Throughout Africa, protracted liberation struggles were being waged against settler colonialism. Many countries in Africa were given 'flag independence.' In North America the civil rights/human rights struggle had taken centre stage as well as the anti-Vietnam war effort. Throughout the Third World the revolutionary fires of Cuba, Korea and Vietnam were burning brightly. Indeed, this was a period of fervent anti-imperialism and anti-capitalism among the dispossessed countries of the world.

The world itself was in the grip of powerful currents. Kwame Nkrumah had broken the back of British Imperialism in Africa. Earlier Nasser had nationalized the Suez canal. Nehru and Tito had already rejected the cold war definition of the world which Truman and Stalin, and afterwards, Eisenhower and Kruschev had sought to impose. They declared neutralism as the guiding principles of foreign policy. . . . In place of the struggle between freedom and communism or capitalism and socialism, the fundamental contradiction in the world was recast as one between former coloniser and formerly colonised, rich and poor, imperialism and national liberation. The idea of the Third World was in the making. These developments were followed with tremendous interest in the Caribbean.[1]

In the Caribbean, this period witnessed the granting of nominal independence to some English-speaking countries. These countries received "briefcase" independence, without any militant anti–colonial struggle. The commanding heights of the economy were still controlled by the merchant/planter elite and foreign multinational corporations. However, the conditions of the masses remained quite stark, because independence did not realize any transformation in their condition. They still suffered grave wretchedness and deprivation. Against this background, a movement emerged calling itself the People's Progressive Movement (PPM). The PPM subscribe to Marxist ideology and saw itself as an alternative party to the Barbados Labour Party (BLP) and the Democratic Labour Party(DLP).[2] Some of the leading members of this party like Bobby Clarke, Calvin Alleyne and John Connell had been exposed to progressive thought and organization whilst studying in Britian. Leroy Harewood, who became the editor of the *Black Star*, the PPM's mouthpiece, had been actively involved in the Black struggle in England, editing a paper called the Monthly Torch.[3] The PPM was also made up of Glenroy Straughn who had recently left the ranks of the BLP, while Ossie Redman, Tyrone Evelyn and Henderson Adams were some of the other leading members of this Party.

It is of great significance that this organ of the PPM was called the *Black Star*. The name the Black Star is of great significance to Pan-Africanism. Garvey's historic shipping line was the called the Black Star. Also, Kwame Nkrumah's Ghana was called the Black Star because she had lighted the path of Africa to independence and the unification of the continent. The primary objective of the *Black Star* newspaper was "to enlighten the masses of Barbados and the wider Caribbean." Moreover the *Black Star* was created "to articulate the concerns of the masses in the Caribbean and to challenge the monopolistic grip of the foreign press and the hegemony of capitalist ideas."

First and foremost it is born to represent that larger section of Barbadians and indeed our brothers and sisters scattered throughout the Caribbean who are finding themselves more and more unrepresented both by the so-called elected representatives and by the various newspapers in their midst that are the monopoly of one man—a foreigner or the mouthpiece of big business.

We believe that if a people are to be politically and socially conscious of the problems that confront them it is imperative that they be given the opportunity to hear a different voice than that of the business tycoon and the political stooge. It is for this reason that *Black Star* has arisen.[4]

This paper espoused a form of revolutionary Black Nationalism. Revolutionary Black Nationalism is a fusion of militant Black Nationalism and Marxism- Leninism, where race and class factors are creatively utilized to explain black exploitation and degradation. The proponents of revolutionary Black Nationalism believed that a structural transformation in society from capitalism to socialism was a necessary prerequisite in ending exploitation and racism. At this juncture it became quite fashionable to link black liberation with socialism and capitalism with oppression and exploitation.[5] Huey Newton argued that to be a revolutionary nationalist you would by necessity have to be a socialist.[6] While Stokeley Carmichael at the Third Annual Black Power Conference had told blacks to reject capitalism.[7] Walter Rodney was of the view that the "goal of our international activity is to develop a perspective that is anti-capitalist, anti-imperialist, and that speaks to the exploitation and oppression of all people."[8] Frantz Fanon, the Pan-African revolutionary was quite emphatic that:

Capitalist exploitation and cartels and monopolies are the enemies of the underdeveloped countries. On the one hand the choice of a socialist regime, a regime which is completely oriented towards the people as a whole and based on the principle that man is the most precious of all possessions will allow us to go forward more quickly and more harmoniously, and thus make impossible that caricature of society where all the economic and political power is held in the hands of a few who regard the nation as a whole with scorn and contempt.[9]

Leroy Harewood after a careful analysis of the Barbadian landscape reached the conclusion "that something was radically wrong with Barbados." He felt that the "cultural, political and economic system is gangrene." He deduced that ninety five percent of the 70,000 acres of arable land is in the hands of a few people. The majority of the banks, insurance companies, utilities companies and hotels were either foreign owned or partly owned by foreign capitalists. The black population ever since the days of slavery has provided the wealth of the country without sharing in the fruits of their labour. The bulk of the wealth ended up in a few hands. He felt that the only way to move away from the present situation was to change the present economic and political system so as to enable the worker to benefit. He felt that it should be known that this "system" was responsible for the slave trade, racism and monoculture agriculture in the various islands. According to Harewood, all of the big businesses must be taken over, and run in the interest of the people. Moreover, the plantation system which has been the cause of so much misery and suffering should be completely "liquidated and the land distributed to the agricultural workers."[10]

Leroy Harewood stated:

But it is only under an entirely new system that the hopes and aspirations of our people can be met. In other words, it is only under a real socialist system that we can conquer the miserable legacy of poverty and backwardness. It is only under a socialist system that the longing hopes of our people for a better life would be realized.[11]

Bobby Clarke asserted that:

> It is not incidental that the companies that control the life-blood of the poor black masses of Barbados happen to be white. It has been the historic policy in Barbados for the white to be a closed unit exploiting the black. . . . The result of this is that we have a capitalist controlled island in which 90 percent of the capitalists are white and the other 10 percent are black with the adverse proportion of white workers and white capitalists.
>
> In light of the above we must understand that socialism is the 'ism', which will usher in a new era. Socialists must adhere to the principles, which they say they believe in. . . . The continuation of a policy desired to gather wealth into the hands of the few capitalists be they black or white, can only create hardships for the poor.[12]

The PPM/The *Black Star* newspaper saw it's mission as:

> . . . fighting for the full coming into their own of the people of the third world. . . . We are fighting to establish the unquestioned dignity of the black man; we are against the dictatorship of capitalism, against exploitation by international capitalism. We are fighting for the redistribution of the national resources for the benefit of the masses.[13]

However, the perceptive Calvin Alleyne recognized that this struggle would not be an easy one because of 300 years of plantation influence and brain washing. He opines that many persons have sub-consciously accepted inferiority; therefore, the first hurdle was to enlighten the masses concerning the harsh realities of their situation. Additionally, to ascertain what was responsible for their present condition so that the people "will suddenly find themselves in a hurry to come into their own to assert themselves, intolerant of any humbug from the smug white race." Therefore, the *Black Star* publications and the PPM were "here to nag the consciences of the masses" and "to bring a new awareness of their dignity, an awareness that the world belongs to them too and that they should not cringe and beg for crumbs."[14]

The PPM/*Black Star* took up the challenge and sought to tackle many of the falsifications and misconceptions that were still prevalent about persons of African extraction. Tyrone Evelyn in a very provocative piece stated that it is generally accepted throughout Barbados and the Caribbean that the black man will never unite. According to him, this line of argument was usually advanced to demonstrate that the black man is no good and he is always fighting against himself. However, Evelyn argued that if we accept this thesis we could safely say that the black man's main reason for this behaviour is motivated because he is primarily interested in self-preservation. Therefore, disunity is the obvious resultant effect of this cause. He was of the view that before starting to condemn we must retrace our history to find the cause of our present thoughts and actions.[15]

Evelyn asserts that this type of indoctrination produced a black slave with a white mentality. Therefore when we hear a black man say that he will never unite with another black man to do something for their common good one must be patient with that particular person because he is still suffering from the effects of the slave mentality and the corrupt plantation society. Moreover, the ignorance of not wanting to accept that they are black and have their own identity is the core of the problem. Evelyn emphatically stated that the division lies in the failure of the black man to accept himself. Re-educating the people can solve this problem so to enable them to know who they are, and where they come from. They must know their history and culture so that they will realize that we are one people with one destiny, and the unity to which we all aspire could become a reality.[16]

In an article entitled "Youth Speak Out," the call was made for an intense study of our history to ascertain that "we are of African Origin, a race of which we can be proud." To discover "How we were stolen from Africa to become the backbone of the European Industrial Revolution, and taught a European culture, which has turned us into idiots."[17] This call was also made by Glenroy Straughn who stated "that West Indians in general and Barbadians in particular are products of a mis-educational system that has provided many avenues for massive cultural erosion." Moreover, Straughn argued that we have given our children hardly anything to build upon except a veneer of Anglo-Saxon prejudices. [18]

Walter Rodney stated:

Every society has a history and a form of culture, and this includes Africa. Africans in the West have been deliberately kept ignorant of their achievements by the white men for centuries. The purpose of their policy was to build up a picture of a barbarous Africa, so that we Africans who have been removed from our homes and made into slaves would be afraid to admit that we were Africans.[19]

Moreover he stated:

One of the major dilemmas inherent in the attempt by black people to break through the cultural aspects of white imperialism is that posed by the use of historical knowledge as a weapon in our struggle. . . . The white man has already implanted numerous historical myths in the minds of Black peoples; those have to be uprooted, since they can act as a drag on revolutionary action in the present epoch. . . . Firstly, the effort must be directed solely towards freeing and mobilising black minds. . . . Secondly, the acquired knowledge of African history must be seen as directly relevant but secondary to the concrete tactics and strategy which are necessary for our liberation.[20]

While Marcus Garvey had stated many years before:

White Historians and writers have tried to rob the black man of his proud past in history and when anything new is discovered to support the race's claim and attest to the

truthfulness of our greatness in other ages, it is skilfully re-
arranged and credited to some other unknown race or people.[21]

Leroy Harewood, in a series of articles entitled, "Who are
We?" sought to educate the masses about their proud history. He
argued that black people are descendants of Africans who were
torn from their homeland and brought by European marauders
to work as slaves on the sugar plantations. Harewood continues
that "we are a people who had a culture and were a proud people in the process of building perhaps the world's greatest civilization." "Now almost everywhere today the black man is made
to feel inferior or related to a second-class citizen." Furthermore,
"wherever the black man and the white man meet the black man
has been forced to conform to the white man's culture." Indeed,
"the white man has inflated and distorted his own importance."
"Everything white is good and every thing black is bad." In addition "Europe and North America are made to look like the cradles
of civilization, while Asia and Africa are considered as the lands
of the backward races." "What is even more distressing is that the
white man has succeeded in making millions of Africans accept
this lie."[22]

Harewood, using the Du Bois thesis asserted that in the four-
teenth century the level of culture in Black Africa south of the Sudan was equal to that of Europe and was so recognized. Moreover, he pointed out that the Negroid influence in the valley of the
Nile was the main influence in Egyptian development from 2100
to 1600 B.C, while in East, South and West Africa, human culture
had from 1600 B.C to A.D 1500 monuments of a vigorous past and
a growing future. Harewood blamed slavery and the slave trade
for wrecking African civilization and blighting African advancement.[23]

Harewood argued that while the voyage from Africa was particularly horrific (with black men and black women forced to remain in stench, squalor and misery being slashed to death, and
thrown overboard). These crimes pale in significance to the ones
committed against the Africans when they landed in the West In-

dies. It was here that the African was stripped of his culture, degraded, and dehumanised. It was here that thingification of the African took place and he was made into a thing, a pitiable human object, knowing no country, owing no loyalty to any man but to the brutal slave master. The primary weapon used by the white man in this process was sheer brutality. This brutality was physical as well as psychological it bred fear, docility, childishness and the lack of self-confidence in the minds of the African.[24] Edmund D'Auivergene in human livestock wrote:

> It was asserted in Parliament in 1780 in Bridgetown, General Tottenham saw a Negro youth entirely naked that wore round his neck an iron collar with five long projecting spikes. His belly and thighs were almost cut to pieces with running ulcers all over them and a finger might have been laid in every one of the wounds. He could not sit down because his hinder parts were mortified and it was impossible for him to lie down on account of the prongs on his collar. He had nearly been whipped to death and then abandoned. [25]

Harewood was of the view that slavery for the black man was something more degrading than being flogged and having to work from morning until night. He felt that there was something more sinister and far more deadly at work on the plantations in the Diaspora. According to him, this was the first time in the history of the human race that a group of people was trying to reduce another group to brutes fit only to work and weep. While Africans were not the only peoples enslaved it was the first time that slavery was associated with a race of people. Moreover, the Africans became slaves forever. Indeed, while the physical chains might be taken away from their ankles they were placed on their minds. The seasoning period was aimed at making the African permanently inferior to the European. Thus while slavery was legally abolished the damage to the black man's psyche was complete. It is this damage that we must seek to repair. Unless this task is accomplished the black man will remain a pariah in the Western World.[26]

Ossie Redman mentioned that the "African is an alien even in his own country because he is not the master of his destiny economically or in terms of social advancement." His oppressors control all the natural resources. Even the culture that has remained on the continent is being overrun by a foreign culture. Throughout the Diaspora the African has lost his cultural identity and is ashamed of his hair and skin colour. What was shameful is that very often-black people were instructed to turn their back on the past, and to view themselves with shame. However, Redman asserts that a thorough knowledge of our history will show us it is not the history of enslavement but our cowardly attitude today. Our leaders, he felt, "were to blame because they never sought to promote any nationalistic fervour that has for centuries heralded the birth of liberation, because for too often they have scoffed at attempts to restore the pride of our race."[27]

The *Black Star* sought to promote pride in blackness. The paper attacked the idea that lighter skins and straight noses in women were beautiful and those who lacked those characteristics were ugly. Ava Turner, in an article entitled "Black Women and Beauty," argued that no other ethnic group degrades itself like the black race. Many Blacks were uncomfortable with their hair, nose and complexion. She believed that it was pathetic that these ideas still persisted. African women, Turner asserted, should be proud of their African beauty because no matter how hard they tried they cannot Europeanise themselves. Moreover, she felt that black women look extremely ugly wearing white women's wigs. Furthermore, no white woman would wear the wigs of Africans with such pride as we wear the wigs of Europeans because they think that their hair is superior to ours. Therefore, if black women are going to wear European hair they must be admitting that such hair is more beautiful than theirs.[28]

The Reverend O.C. Haynes deplored the lack of real black pride among a large segment of the black population who disliked the colour of their skins. He stressed that God could not use individuals who were annoyed with the way they were born. Haynes believed that there was no reason why black people could not have a black Virgin Mary because the Indians have an Indian Virgin Mary. He blamed the educational system for teaching Blacks to be inferior, and to ape the Europeans, as "if the only way to heaven was through the European door."[29] Garvey had stated that if man was created in the image and likeness of God, then black people should depict a God in their own image, which would inevitably be black.[30] Frances Welshing the psychiatrist stated quite emphatically:

> To be black and accept consciously or unconsciously the image of God as a white man is the highest possible form of self-negation and lack of self-respect under the specific conditions of white domination. Such perception, emotional response and thought are therefore insane. This logic circuit ensures that Black people always will look up to white people and, therefore, down upon themselves. Only by breaking that logic circuit can the concept of Black and other non-white liberation become a reality.[31]

Ossie Redman believed that changes had been taking place in the thought processes of many black men/women. He recognized that many of them had started to come to a greater awareness of themselves; and that pride in being black had started to take root. In some cases the self-hatred that they felt for their hair and skin had started to decline. While he gave *Black Star* and The Socialist Youth Movement some credit for this development, he recognized this was also influenced by what was happening throughout the African world. Redman was aware that the struggle taking place was not only political but also cultural and many "Uncle Toms" were seeking to exploit the black is beautiful look which they viewed as a new fad. However, he remarked 'that the image and struggle of the black man is no laughing matter, no gimmick to be played, for it is a struggle for self respect of a people long denied the inalienable right of justice and equality.'[32]

The PPM/*Black Star*, unlike the other political parties in Barbados, sought to place the question of true independence firmly on the agenda. The PPM recognized that neo-colonialism was entrenching itself and they felt that the onus was on the government to take the helm and usher in a new era for the benefit of the masses. It was ludicrous that on the eve of independence the Barbados Police Force's name was changed to the Royal Barbados Police Force. In addition, government had made no pronouncements on abolishing colonial trappings such as knighthoods, Queens Counsel (QC) and the Order of the British Empire (OBE). John Connell in the Fanonist mould wondered if the National Anthem was just a "sterile litany." He raised several questions about its relevance. Is it really relevant to our experience as a people? As a statement of history is it accurate? As a prognosis of the future is it realistic?[33]

'In plenty and in time of need
when this fair land was young
our brave forefathers sowed the seeds.'
When precisely were these times?
Brave forefathers must refer either to the white
slave masters or the black slaves or both.
To speak of the time in need in relation to the former is a misuse of the words. As for the slave, the only plenty he knew was work and hard lashes.
What seed did these contending classes sow—The Sugar Plantation? This there only partnership was a relationship of rider and horse.
The pride of Nationhood binds our heart from coast to coast. Indeed in spite of this mythical link, the wealthy whites live on the plush west and south coast. The bulk of the blacks are herded inland in slums and tenantries, like parallel lines they never meet.
We loyal sons and daughters
Loyal to whom? And why?
Do hereby make it Known,
These fields and hill beyond recall

Are now our very own.
What if any thing are these lines saying? Are they a decla-
ration that since 30th November 1966 the large sugar plan-
tations are now vested in the people of Barbados?
We write our name on history pages
with expectations great—
Great expectations of what? New outlets for domestics,
greater U.S involvement in Barbadian life.
The Lord has been the people's guide
With him still on the peoples side
We have no doubt or fears
Which Lord? The same Lord as the Bishop of Lincoln who
demanded every red cent for his black slaves emancipa-
tion.
Upward and onward we shall go
Inspired exalting free
Free from what? The foreign banks, insurance compa-
nies?
Tell me is our anthem really relevant to our experience or
is it a sterile litany.[34]

Leroy Harewood wondered if independence was "nothing but
a fancy dress parade and the blare of trumpets," with "nothing
save a fancy re-adoption, a few reforms at the top and down there
at the bottom an undivided mass, still living in the middle ages,
endlessly marking time."[35] Connell asked 'whether independence
go deeper than a mere formal transfer of responsibility from day
to day government from Britain to our locally elected Barbadian
leaders'? Or whether it was an "expensive show, a concerted effort
to dupe the masses into believing whether they were really free?"
He argued that the countries of Latin America received formal independence over 150 years ago, "but none of these countries had
banished the spectre of unemployment, slum housing, starvation
wages and unbearable high prices. In none of these countries has
power been transferred to the working class who comprised the
largest segment of the population. According to Connell, only

when this is done will independence be meaningful."[36]

Leroy Harewood in an article entitled "Why is there Under-development?" He wondered whether there was some evil god that ordains poverty, hunger and misery for millions and riches for the few? According to Harewood for centuries the nations of Africa, Asia and Latin America had been mercilessly plundered by European marauders under the rubric of colonialism and im-perialism.[37] This position was shared by the dependency school, especially Walter Rodney in his magisterial work "How Europe Underdeveloped Africa," where he saw a direct nexus between Africa's underdevelopment and Europe's development.[38]

Frantz Fanon was brutally frank when he stated that:

> This European opulence is literally scandalous, for it has been founded on slavery, it has been nourished with the blood of slaves and it comes directly from the soil and subsoil of that underdeveloped world. The well-being and progress of Europe have been built up with the sweat and dead bodies of the Negroes, Arabs, Indians and the yellow races.[39]

Harewood pointed out that the nations of the economic South are extremely rich, but their peoples are poor because they are exploited by the economic North. Although these countries are independent they still provided the raw materials for the indus-trialized world. He argued that the following devices were used to maintain underdevelopment in the new-colonies:

1. Puppet governments propped-up by arms from North Amer-ica and Europe and installed in most countries in Africa, Asia, Latin America and the Caribbean.
2. Big banks, insurance companies and foreign firms moved into most of these countries to mop up finance and cheap labour.
3. No real development is allowed except the building of tourist resorts, a few window-dressing projects like a housing area, a new post office, a new highway or a new school.

4. There is no agricultural development.
5. Money borrowed from foreign banks at exorbitant rates of interest to line the pockets of venal corrupt politicians and trade union leaders.
6. A high level of unemployment is maintained to provide cheap docile labour for subsidiaries of big North American firms.
7. A one-crop economy forms the hub of most of the hungry countries. And this one crop whether it is sugar, coffee or bananas is controlled by a handful of capitalists, sometimes foreign, sometimes local and foreign. The main point is that none of them is interested in the development of the country.
8. Many of the countries insist on trading mainly with Britain, the United States and Canada. Any trade with Eastern Europe is frowned upon; more often it is deliberately stopped.
9. The primary products of the underdeveloped countries are bought by the developed countries for next to nothing. Yet they sell these countries their manufactured goods at very high prices.
10. Ways and means are found to crush all local initiative and keep the people dependent on foreigners, from everything from the making of a pin to the running of a hospital.[40]

Harewood felt that the same worn and old paths left by the imperialists could not eliminate poverty and hunger. Additionally, he felt that poverty could not be conquered by waiting on handouts from abroad. What the countries of the periphery need to do was to pool their human and material resources in order to become less dependent on the imperialists. Hunger therefore, could definitely be conquered but the first step in the process was to conquer neo-colonialism and colonialism.[41]

The PPM/*Black Star* believed that if the below charter was followed then Barbadian masses would receive genuine rights:

1. Smash the plantation system. Give land to the landless agricultural workers to be worked under a strict cooperative system directed by trained agricultural officers.

2. Control all the banks and banking.
3. Nationalize all insurance companies.
4. Slash all prices and implement rigid price control, with severe penalties for anyone who tries to fleece the people.
5. Raise the wages of all manual labourers.
6. Slash the salaries of all top civil servants and MPs and abolish the unnecessary office of Governor-General.
7. Ask the Yankees to remove their bases and all other war like installations on Barbadian soil.
8. Start tearing down the slums and carry out a gigantic building programme to provide homes for the homeless.
9. Stop teaching one-way religious knowledge to our children and introduce a study of comparative religions.
10. Tear down all imperialist statues and rename all the streets.
11. Stop Yankee cultural imperialism in films, books and religious broadcasts.
12. Open diplomatic, trade and cultural relationships with all countries, especially Africa and Asia.
13. Ask Eric Williams to lift the ban on literature.
14. Condemn the fraudulent Guyana elections.
15. Condemn the Jamaican government for its ban on literature.
16. Control the tourist industry and bring all hotels under public ownership.
17. Nationalize all public utilities- electricity and the telephone.
18. Stop selling Barbadian land to foreigners.
19. Wherever possible avoid using arable land for building purposes.
20. Abolish the so-called independent schools by introducing free education for all.
21. Provide full employment for all and stop the drain of young people and talent away from this country to racist countries.[42]

The *Black Star* sought to sensitize its readers about the various anti-colonial and anti-imperialist struggles occurring worldwide, particularly the liberation struggles in Africa. The paper in the spirit of proletarian internationalism paid homage to Che Guevara the great revolutionary leader who was killed in Bolivia. The *Black Star*/PPM labelled him, as "the greatest freedom fighter the world has ever known." In addition, the paper took the position that words were inadequate to express the debt that suffering humanity owes to this great liberator, who was prepared to give his life so that they might be free from centuries of misery and backwardness. The paper reminded its readers of his speech at the United Nations General Assembly when he attacked the racist regime in South Africa.[43] He stated:

> . . . Once again we raise our voice to put the world on guard against what is happening in South Africa. The brutal policy of apartheid is being carried out before our very eyes. . . . The people of Africa are being compelled to tolerate in that continent the concept of the superiority of one race over another and in the name of racial superiority they murder the people with impunity . . .[44]

The *Black Star* was firm in its condemnation of the illegal racist regime in Rhodesia. The paper was outraged at the ongoing hangings of the freedom fighters by the Ian Smith regime. It viewed this as open war against global Africa. The paper arrived at the position that when the so-called western democracies talk about freedom and the free world they excluded the people of colour throughout the world. The lead writer viewed the killings in the same vein as the mass killings taking place in Vietnam. Moreover, he believed the time for platitudes was over and African peoples must "practice an eye for an eye and a life for a life." Any other course will be genocidal.[45] In a piece entitled 'West Indians denounce Smith-Wilson savage acts of murder' the writer stated:

> Ian Smith in his scornful contempt for world opinion and rights of African people of Zimbabwe who constitute the majority of the population has raised the indignation of the African people, and the people of African descent throughout the world and has heightened our determina-

tion to fight more resolutely to drive the colonialist out of the last racist outpost of Africa to win complete liberation for the people of African descent in the United States of America, in the West Indies and wherever they have been scattered by imperialism.

. . . Since the illegal Smith regime is uniting with the fascist regimes of South Africa and Portugal, and is being covertly assisted by the British and American imperialism, Africa must now close their ranks, oppressed black people throughout the world must do like wise and together with other revolutionary peoples intensify their struggle against imperialism, colonialism, racism and fascism and strengthen their solidarity against these common enemies.[46]

In another hard hitting piece entitled 'The Double Dealing of the West' the *Black Star* emphatically stated that the protestations of the western governments against the atrocities in Rhodesia were sheer hypocrisy. They felt that since 11 November 1965 the Wilson government in Britain had pussyfooted and allowed the Smith regime to consolidate and tighten his grip on the seized territory. Alex Hume, the former British Prime Minister, saw this "as a matter of white kith and kin versus blacks." While these countries speak about force and sanctions against Rhodesia, behind their backs 'they pass a slimy hand to Ian Smith for filthy lucre'! These countries had only one creed, according to the *Black Star*, and that was Western Europe Must Flourish; at the expense of Africa if necessary. It was clear that the British government was morally too decrepit to apply force, thus economic sanctions alone could not remove the racist illegal regime in Rhodesia. Economic sanctions would not work because Rhodesian beef and copper were still coming to Britain. In France a centre called UNIVEX had been set up to distribute beef, tobacco, and metals from Rhodesia to West Germany, Holland, Belgium, Switzerland and throughout France itself. The *Black Star* felt that nothing but violence "can tear the leeches of Europe away from the arteries of Africa and dash them to the ground." They felt that the only sensible option left was all out war.[47]

The PPM waged an intense campaign against the apartheid regime in South Africa and fought valiantly against an invitation from the Barbados Cricket Association (BCA) to three South African cricketers–Colin Bland and Peter and Graeme Pollock, to join a Rest of the World team to play against Barbados as part of its independence celebration. This invitation was subsequently withdrawn in January 1967.[48] The *Black Star* informed its readers of the Basil D'Oliviera issue when the South Africans refused to play against the English cricket team because he was said to be coloured. The paper felt that D'Oliveria was being knocked about by the British and South African racists. "South Africa is a racist regime, where all the imperialist countries have some interest and have agreed to ensure the economic and military developments so as to ensure that South Africa continues to support Portugal's attempts to hold onto Mozambique and Angola and to give open patronage to the fascist Ian Smith regime."[49]

The PPM/ *Black Star* as a victim of repression was very hostile against the repression that was sweeping the Caribbean and North America. John Connell mentions that:

> all territories including Barbados there is the increasing and unsavoury tendency for the police to breathe down the necks of persons who dare to express views that the establishment does not like. Public meetings are tape-recorded. Persons selling and buying progressive journals and literature are constantly questioned and harassed. [50]

In Trinidad, the reactionary Eric Williams regime sought to ban all progressive literature. Moreover, the Trinidadian government refused to give Stokely Carmichael and his wife Miriam Makeba permission to enter the land of his birth. They also sought to introduce the Industrial Stabilization Act to suppress the natural aspirations of the working classes. In Jamaica, the government withdrew the passports of Dr. Taylor and Dr. Beckford and expelled Walter Rodney from the island. [51]

The *Black Star* gave solidarity to Huey Newton and Rap Brown, two imprisoned leaders of the Black Panther Party, and provided its readers with information and articles on the leading Black figures and updates on how the Black Struggle was unfolding in the U.S.A. as well as in Africa. With articles such as We going to be free By any Means by Rap Brown, Message from Jail by Rap Brown, Black Panthers to arms, Frantz Fanon: The Great West Indian Revolutionary, Mozambique a People Determined to Fight, Nyerere Arm Youth, Malcolm X in Retrospective, Black Panther and the US Establishment, Black Power and the Revolutionary Struggle by Huey Newton, Nkrumah Myth and Reality, Negritude and World revolution by Walter Rodney were some of the articles that educated the Barbadian public.

The PPM was firmly behind the Caribbean students who had protested at the Sir George Williams University in Canada against the professor who the students said was a racist—who was giving black students poor grades. They were involved in a demonstration to force the university authorities to take some action against racism and were arrested for their actions. A number of Barbadian and Caribbean nationals were arrested. The PPM held a public meeting where they sought to enlighten the public about the events at George Williams and why the students resorted to the action they took. Leroy Harewood "linked the struggle of Caribbean students in Canada to the universal struggles of Black oppressed peoples everywhere for freedom." He felt that 'the students struggle against Canadian racism is only one part of the big global struggle of Black men and women for their rights'.[52] Glenroy Straughn and Leroy Harewood told the people that they could not afford to remain isolated from what was going on in the world. Racism is an evil that must be fought; its roots lie in imperialism and capitalism.[53]

The *Black Star* sought to defend the hallowed name of Kwame Nkrumah arguably the greatest Pan-Africanist, who was overthrown in Ghana. The paper pointed out that the imperialists and their black stooges throughout the world have constantly maligned Kwame Nkrumah. They accused him of being a tyrant who had brought nothing but suffering to the people since independence. However, it was Nkrumah's call for African unity that the imperialists feared. They knew that as long as Africa remains Balkanized it will remain weak and impotent. Therefore, they sought to destroy him. Nkrumah, like Garvey before him, declared Africa for the Africans therefore, he had to be crushed. Thus, the capitalists and neo- colonialists began to spread all types of falsehood about Nkrumah. His faults were exaggerated and his mistakes were regarded as being criminal attacks upon the people.[54]

The *Black Star* featured articles by Nkrumah. In one such article Nkrumah sought to define what was Black Power. He was of the view that Black Power in the United States is part of the vanguard of the world revolution against capitalism, imperialism and neo-colonialism, which has enslaved and oppressed peoples everywhere. According to him, Black Power is taking place throughout Africa and its Diaspora and it is linked with the Pan-African struggle for the unity of the African continent with those who are fighting to establish a socialist society. Nkrumah felt that Black Power is a black vanguard movement that is pointing the way for all the oppressed masses. Moreover, he viewed the liberation struggles in Africa as the triumph of the human spirit, the collapse of the forces of inhumanity and the glorious effort to liberate humanity from an inhumane and senseless exploitation, from degradation and war. Nkrumah felt that the old Africa is crumbling and a new Africa was being built. In Africa we thought we could achieve freedom and independence and our final objectives unity and socialism, by peaceful means. However, he admitted that this strategy has placed us in the power of neo-colonialism. We cannot triumph by using non-violent methods. The same power that is hindering the Afro-American struggle is also placing obstacles in Africa's path. Imperialism, neo-colonialism and racism are trying to overcome and subjugate us. Thus we must struggle wherever neo-colonialism, imperialism and racism exist. It is necessary to understand that liberation movements in Africa, the black power struggle in America or in any part of the world, can only be consummated in the political unification of Africa, the homeland of the Blackman and the descendants of Africa throughout the world. [55]

The *Black Star* allowed Walter Rodney, the leading Pan-African theoretician in the Caribbean, to have a voice in explaining what was happening in Jamaica and in the wider black world. Rodney recognized that black intellectuals are as much a part of the white capitalist system as the bank managers and plantation overseers. Their position is secure on the condition that they make no meaningful contact with the Black masses. He felt that the black intellectual is also more dehumanised than the black brother in the street because he is more completely a paper representation of what the white man wants us all to be.[56] He felt that three possibilities existed for the black intellectuals to break out of this Babylonian captivity:

1. To attack wherever possible the distortions produced by white cultural imperialism in his own field of study.
2. To launch an attack against all social myths which seek to destroy the identity and creativity of the black masses.
3. The conscious black man must attach himself at all times to the activities of the black people seeking emancipation.[57]

Rodney felt that our West Indian societies virtually invented racism. It was on the slave plantations that the fantastic socioeconomic gulf which existed between black and white came to be rationalized and accepted as the natural order of things. The white man viewed his property (black people) and rated them little higher than the animals on the plantations. He felt that he was innately superior and the Blackman inherently inferior. They developed pseudo-scientific and theological theories, which were supposed to prove the inferiority of Africans. Rodney made the assertion that Africans have already performed a miracle of survival. We are very alive with culture and vitality. Whatever is worthwhile and creative in the West Indies has come from the black sufferers and they will ultimately prevail.[58]

The *Black Star* was effectively destroyed when it was announced that all newspapers in Barbados would have to pay a registration fee of $100. Unlike its competitors, the *Black Star* did not carry any advertisements on its pages to raise revenue; this was dictated by its anti-capitalist stance. Therefore, this fee was an additional burden that the paper could not afford. Indeed, the PPM members saw this development as being directly targeted against the *Black Star* to silence the voice of protest.[59] This voice was effectively silenced when its headquarters was destroyed by fire. To many of its readers the *Black Star* was responsible for light- ing the path of black consciousness that was crystallized in the Black Power movement in the island. Beyond a shadow of a doubt the *Black Star* contributed to black dignity and Pan-African con- sciousness in Barbados.

The PPM's demise quickly followed the death of the *Black Star*. The bye-election in the city in 1969 represented the final straw that effectively destroyed the PPM. The editorial entitled 'Democracy' raised questions about democracy: i) whether the politically ig- norant, the debauched and the corrupt who are prepared to sell their votes for a few cents can be in the position to determine the destiny of progressive people who honestly and sincerely believe in the economic, social and cultural advancement of their coun- try? ii) Why should some mindless drunkard who boasts about receiving money for his vote be allowed to go to the polls and put an x against his name? Leroy Harwood felt that this was not democracy but madness.[60]

In an article "A vote to break their own necks":

The city by–elections in May 1969 is now history. The peo- ple have cast their votes, the political hacks and termites are now at rest waiting in their holes and slime until they are called forth again by our noble rulers to perform yet another task of misinforming, corrupting and perverting the minds of the people.

However the masses have made their decisions ignor- ing the facts and figures and pour scorn on progress the people of the city have again sold themselves down the stench hole. They have again shown that they prefer mis-

ery and squalor, unemployment and starvation . . . ignorance and filth to enlightenment, cleanliness and economic
and social advancement.

The Peoples Progressive Movement presented a candi-
date that offered the people of the city a unique chance
from the sort of misrepresentation they have had for over
23 years. Every social and economic question that affects
their lives was dealt with ranging from bad housing, cost
of living to education and tourism. Never before in the history of this island had a political party done so much to
open the eyes of the people to the harsh realities of life.

What we of the PPM tried to do was to make the people
understand the truth and to strip away all pretence and
make belief. We failed because of the deep inferiorization
of our people. And in this respect the people have also
failed.[61]

While the movement was reconstituted and continued to function until 1973, vigorously promoting the Black Power philosophy,
it had lost many of its leading members. Calvin Alleyne stated:

that the biggest cause for the demise is that we were not
getting the response that we hoped for, so it frustrated us.
While we were formed as a political party, with the rise of
the Black Power Movement in the United States, people
came to associate us more as Black Power advocates than
as a mainstream political party. This helped to stymie the
growth of the party. A sense of futility beset us and some of
the comrades decided to make a contribution within other
political parties.[62]

Munford argued that:

There is a political precept, which sets a time limit within which any revolutionary political party must achieve
power and consolidate the intended social transformation.

Thereafter degeneration is inevitable, with or with out the achievement of the goal . . . if it does not achieve power within a single generation, then impetuous ardour gives way to opportunism and careerism.[63]

The reasons given for the demise of the PPM are i) co-option; ii) frustration (not being able to gain any significant number of votes, far less seats in the electoral process; iii) personality clashes especially on tactics and strategies; iv) political naivety (the belief that naked oppression and poverty was the raison d'être to awaken a people to a sense of struggle, v) organizational weaknesses (Bobby Clarke is of the view that the major shortcoming of the PPM was not grounding sufficiently with the people;[64] vi) financial hardships; vii) and repression and harassment best manifested in the Public Order Act, which was specifically aimed to curb the activities of the PPM and prevent the people from spontaneously assembling. Calvin Alleyne believed that 'the Public Order Act was created in an apparent attempt to clamp down on their meetings. We used to hold weekly meetings all over the island. We were not waiting for elections to hold meetings'. We were spreading the message and activating people.[65] Bobby Clarke also shared this view.

In the debate on the Public Order Act Bernard St. John stated:

. . . I believe I am right in saying that the sole purpose of bringing this bill before the chamber is purely to prevent and stop the spread of Black Power in the West Indies. . . . The government through this bill is trying to kill and emasculate the dignity and self-respect of the young black people of this country.[66]

Eyre Hoppin stated:

This Government is not against the Black Power Movement as that member has said, . . . we are not running underground, as has been suggested, to come up again, but everything should be done in a proper way. If Trinidad had a Public Order Act, I am of the opinion that they would not have been in the plight that they are in today.[67]

Tom Adams in his contribution stated:

Nobody is going to follow Bobby Clarke down the road to Jenkins Lunatic Asylum...nobody is going to take on or consider the People's Progressive Movement...because now that it has lost Mr. Connell and Mr. Harewood has gone back to England, the only members the Peoples Progressive Movement have for all of the flattery given to it by Calvin Alleyne's ex-colleagues at the Advocate Newspaper-the only members it has are Mr. Redman, Mr. Allen and Mr. Bobby Clarke and yet it is graced and flattered by the name of a political party. The greatest number of votes I believe any of its candidates ever polled was 120 votes that Mr. Alleyne polled against the Minister of Communications and Works and myself; Mr. Straughn against the honourable Senior member for St. James polled 108 votes, and when we came down to more recent events when the political lines were cut a little shorter, we witnessed the spectacle of the so-called political party polling 32 votes out of many thousands cast in a by election here in the city of Bridgetown, where as they say the poorest and most depressed class of the proletariat live. And yet all up and down St. James, all the persons who came here, from the fly by night businessman to the reputable ones, are worrying their heads because of the political meetings being held by four persons. Alleyne, Bobby Clarke, Redman and Eric Sealy.[68]

It is important to note that Bobby Clarke played an important role in the steering Committee of the Caribbean Pan-Africanists who were preparing for the Sixth Pan-African Congress in Tanzania. According to Kambron, the steering committee met regularly at Bobby's house where they had many enlightened discussions and came to many common positions on issues confronting the Caribbean masses. Indeed, Barbados and Guyana were the only countries in the Caribbean that allowed the Pan-Africanists to come to their shores, because the comrades who went to prison in Trinidad were banned by the reactionary Governments of the Caribbean. It was tragic that these Pan-Africanists from the Caribbean could not attend the congress due to the participation of the governments they were fighting against in the Caribbean. [69]

The PPM/*Black Star* contribution to the growth of a Pan-Africanism in Barbados cannot be overstated. Indeed the seeds of the PPM/Black Star flowered in the Black power Movement and Pan-African formations in the 70s, 80s and indeed the early nineties. Nearly all of the leaders and many of the members were influenced significantly by the work of PPM/*Black Star*. The next chapter will look at Black Night, the Southern African Liberation movement, the Rastafarian movement, the Clement Payne Movement, the Pan-African Movement of Barbados and the Commission of Pan-African Affairs.

5
Pan-Africanism in the Post-1970s

Black Night

Around 1970, there emerged a loose formation, which called itself Black Night. Black Night consisted of some of the more radical poets, actors, musicians and writers of this period who met in Baxter's Road to discuss the main socio-economic and socio-political issues of the day. Elton Elombe Mottley, the director of Youth Rural and Urban of Barbados (YORUBA) describes Black Night as "an experience." "It is the coming together of all those experiences that make us Black." "It is the fear, the trials and the tribulations of the Black man living in a white world of white values".[1]

Mottley, in seeking to clarify the position of Black Night on Black Power stated, "Black Night believes in power to the people because 95 percent of the Barbadian population is black, then power to the people means black power." Black Night believed that true black power could only be achieved when political power is exercised more in the interests of the majority of people. Black Night recognized that one of the greatest myths told to black people is that the attainment of political power equals black power. When the black political elite assumed the governance of the country they did little to change the thinking and attitudes, which encouraged the subservience of black people to white values, white institutions and white ideologies.[2]

Black Night's position closely mirrors that of Walter Rodney who defines black power as "a movement and an ideology springing from the oppression of black peoples by whites within the imperialist world as a whole." According to Rodney, black power is a call to black peoples to throw off white domination and resume the handling of their own destinies. It also meant that Blacks would enjoy power commensurate with their numbers in the world and particular localities. He argued that black power in the West Indies means three closely related things:

1. the break with imperialism which is historically white racist;
2. the assumption of power by the black masses in the islands;
3. the cultural reconstruction of the society in the image of the Blacks.[3]

Stokely Carmichael, one of the leading ideologues on black power, argues   black power is a summons for black people to unite, to recognize their heritage, to build a sense of community. Moreover, he held the view that black power logically leads to Pan-Africanism, and the highest political expression of black power is Pan-Africanism.[4]

Black Night argued that it is imperative that black people seek to redefine themselves. They should no longer accept the definitions of the white man, they must cease to be a nigger and reject the idea that Black people are lazy. In fact, the black powerites asked the people to reject and re-examine all the falsifications propagated about black people. They should replace them with positive affirmations. You are no longer ugly, you are beautiful. Your black kinky hair is good hair. You have a long historical tradition that you should be proud of.[5]

They also argued that the system of capitalism in the West Indies has been developed on the exploitation of black people. Therefore, they wanted to see the co-operative method utilized in business and banking. Black Night envisioned the creation of a society in which the spirit of community and humanistic love would prevail.[6] It must be noted that before the 1967 Black Power conference black power was grounded in communal control, co-operatives and socialism. Capitalism was its nemesis, however, after this conference there was an emergence of a strong pro-capitalist bias as the white corporate elite and the comprador black bourgeoisie hijacked the Black Power slogan.[7] The cry for Black Power by the PPM and the Black Night as well as developments in the Caribbean and North America forced the corporate elite to take stock. They recognized that something would have to be done to appease the black powerites to prevent the violence that was attendant to cries of black power elsewhere. Therefore, the corporate elite started to give some concessions to the black powerites. They embarked on a policy of Black visibility, where more blacks were hired than before in stores and banks and many other jobs that had previously been the preserve of whites. However, the fundamental cry of the Black powerites for land reform and economic democracy went unanswered.[8]

The embryonic black power formation suffered when some of its members including Elombe Mottley and his lieutenant Kofi Akobi joined the Barbados Labour Party. These individuals concentrated on partisan politics to the detriment of the Black Power movement. Moreover, many of the people became satisfied with the tangential victories achieved by Black Power agitation; they believed that they could gradually accomplish their objectives and retreated from the radical tactics of the past.

The Southern African Liberation Committee (SALC)

In the spirit of Pan-African Brotherhood and global African solidarity, an organization was created in Barbados called the Southern African Liberation Committee in 1977. The objectives of SALC were:

1. To carry out educational work in solidarity with the struggles of the liberation fighters of Southern Africa;
2. To organize and coordinate activist campaigning in support of

the liberation movement;

3. To, in any other way, as determined by the executive, render material or moral support and solidarity with the oppressed people of Southern Africa.[9]

SALC, under the astute chairmanship of Michael Cummins, and other leading figures such as Ricky Parris, Harry Husbands, Norman Faria, Claire Kennedy (was involved in the civil rights movement in the United states) and the hardworking, long serving secretary Viola Davis, expressed unity in the struggle and solidarity with the oppressed peoples of Southern Africa and the major organizations—the South West African Peoples Organization (SWAPO) in Namibia and the African National Congress (ANC) in South Africa—involved in the liberation struggles. Claire Kennedy's importance in this organization cannot be over stated because she brought to the SALC several years of involvement in the Civil Rights movement in the United States where she was born until she came to live in Barbados. The SALC was very concerned with the atrocities being meted out to their African brothers and sisters. The SALC's solidarity with the comrades and peoples of South Africa was very similar to the Pan-African solidarity as expressed by Amilcar Cabral:

> ...We know that all African peoples are our brothers. Our struggle is their struggle. Every drop of blood that falls in our countries, fall also from their body and hearts, these African peoples...[10]

Therefore, they sought to sensitize and educate the Barbadian public about the horrors of apartheid - to this end they put out a publication called Sports and Apartheid, in addition to countless letters to the press, lectures and rallies. SALC pointed out that under the apartheid system all of the country's legal, political and economic institutions were firmly based on racial discrimination. Only the minority white population could vote, black workers are paid less than the whites and black women were not even considered as persons under the law.[11]

The SALC, like many Pan-African bodies worldwide expressed solidarity with the black people in South Africa and on the anniversary of the Sharpville Massacre on the 21st March (1960 when 69 people were killed and several hundred injured) in a media release stated:

> To maintain its illegal and racist rule, the various South African governments over the years have had to resort to brutal violence to attempt to crush all opposition both in South Africa, and in neighboring territories. The Sharpville Massacre of March 21st 1960 is but one example of the murderous policy not only against freedom fighters in the African National Congress (ANC) of South Africa and the South West African People's organization (SWAPO) in Namibia, but against unarmed civilians including children.
>
> In recent times we witnessed the brutal and obscene raid on the sovereign nation of Lesotho by South African security forces, an action in which 37 people were shot down in cold blood. Moreover, in addition to the increase in jailings and deaths in prisons at the hands of the authorities, Pretoria's security forces have stepped up its activities to assassinate members and leaders of the ANC and SWAPO.
>
> All Barbadians, regardless of their political affiliations, are urged by SALC to redouble their efforts this year to extend solidarity to those struggling for freedom in South Africa by further helping to build respect for calls by the ANC and SWAPO for a total boycott on all fronts of Pretoria's abhorrent apartheid system. Moreover, more pressure must be put on the Barbadian government to actively support this boycott by refraining, for example, from giving contracts for government work to transnational corporations, which have branch plants in South Africa.[12]

The SALC was firmly of the view that the Barbadian government needed to develop closer ties with the liberation movements SWAPO and the ANC. In addition SALC felt that the Barbadian government should appeal for the release of all political prisoners in South Africa including Nelson Mandela and Walter Sisulu, especially at the United Nations.[13]

The SALC kept the Barbadian public abreast of developments that were unfolding in South Africa especially the atrocities that were being carried out against Black people. This was manifested in several articles they sent to the media houses; articles such as Group Condemns Raids, SALC Condemns Brutal Murders of SA Blacks, SALC Calls on Community to Fight Apartheid, Fascism, and Help those in South Africa. All this was evident in the various discussions and agitation for the comrades in South Africa. In the wake of the imprisonment of Brother Seatholo and his companions the SALC wrote:

> This deed by the South African state has prompted us to renew and reiterate our resolve against fascism and racism. We denounce the brutal practices and oppressive nature of the condemned regime of Pieter Botha and his friends and allies which are being encouraged even more shamelessly than before by the Ronald Reagan government in the United States.
>
> We call for a coordinated assault against the internal and external machinery of the apartheid system to bring an end, once and for all, to the network of hypocrisy and collusion, which allows the apartheid system to continue.
>
> We beseech the government of Barbados to raise the issue for the safety and proper treatment of brother Khotso and other political prisoners and detainees in South Africa.
>
> We further urge our government to respond to this most recent outrage by rallying with the international community to halt and overcome the crime against humanity, which continues to be perpetuated in the form of racism, fascism and apartheid.[14]

The SALC went as far as to write a letter to the South African Government, which read as follows:

The Southern Africa Liberation Committee a community based organization in Barbados, which informs the Barbadian public of developments within Southern Africa, notes with dismay and sorrow the death on January 5th, while in the custody of the South Africa police of the trade unionist Dr. Neil Agget.

The explanation given by your police department that Dr. Aggett had hanged himself cannot be taken seriously by any person who has even a rudimentary knowledge of the type of justice meted out to jailed opponents of the apartheid system within South Africa. We doubt whether Dr. Aggett an elected official of a represented trade union took his own life in the way described by the police.

We are reminded of the death in 1978 in a South African jail of noted student leader Steve Biko.

What is needed now is a special inquiry on Dr. Aggett's death.

It should be an investigation where all the facts about his unfortunate death are placed on the table.

We also urge the release, in the name of justice and humanity, of all political prisoners now languishing in South African jails. Let the patriots free!
Yours truly
Norman Faria
(For the SALC executive)[15]

The SALC waged a relentless campaign to have the Space Research Corp. (SRC) removed from Barbados after it was discovered that this firm was selling munitions to the South Africans. The Canadian government was prompted to investigate the operations of the company after the SALC, the Antigua Liberation Movement (ACLM) and some member countries of the UN started to agitate against this firm when they received information from Joshua Nkomo about the nefarious activities of SRC. The Canadian government discovered that SRC was unlawfully supplying South Africa with gun barrels, projectiles and tracking devices. SRC was ordered to close its operations in Barbados and Antigua.[16] While the SALC commended the BLP government for taking the above action, they felt that the BLP should forge relationships with the newly independent countries in Africa like Zimbabwe. "By forging them they believe it would be possible to give assistance and render ineffective the forces that operate South Africa's weapons on the test range in Barbados."[17]

The SALC, like the ANC, firmly believed that the racist regime could be defeated if the international boycott against the Pretoria regime was successful. When the Guyanese government prevented Robin Jackman from playing in Guyana because he had played cricket in South Africa, this action was totally endorsed by the SALC. Indeed, the SALC condemned the Foreign Ministers who met to determine whether the English tour of the Caribbean would continue. The SALC felt that the ministers were overly concerned about the possibility of isolation if they held a different position. Therefore, they sought a consensus and misread the nature of the issues.[18] The foreign ministers agreed that:

> The point of contention . . . is whether sanctions should be invoked against those members of the (English) team who played cricket in South Africa after the Gleneagles agreement.[19]

The SALC disagreed with this position and stated that they needed to consider:

1. that by selecting Robin Jackman and any others who have played cricket in the racist republic of South Africa since Gleneagles, the English breached both the spirit and letter of agreement;
2. that in so far as it advances the interest of isolating all sporting contacts with South Africa, Guyana's position demands some

measure of support;
3. that the reaction of the English authorities to Guyana's decision in their statement about their right of selection and in unilaterally canceling that leg of the tour constitutes arrogance and disrespect. The English authorities have further asserted their right to flout the Gleneagles agreement.[20]

The SALC felt that that the Caribbean governments had taken a weak willed position since the English had flouted the Gleneagles accord, our policy responses must not be constrained by the limited consensus which Gleneagles achieved. Instead our governments should be inspired to uphold the spirit of Gleneagles and to advance the interest of the cause, which it represents.[21]

The SALC felt that the foreign ministers seemed to be appealing to the stipulations (rather than the spirit) of Gleneagles and the UN declaration of 1977. Thus the Foreign Ministers intended to absolve themselves from treating the current issue on its own merits. By ignoring the specifics they arrived at a solution which did not violate the stipulations of any international documents. The SALC therefore recommended:

1. that governments in the Caribbean should hasten to design their own policy agreement which clearly stipulates a code of conduct in sports with particular reference to the objective of isolating all sporting contacts, direct or indirect, with the racist Republic of South Africa;
2. the current lesson about Gleneagles should be extended to motivate initiatives to introduce a code of conduct for businesses such as Barclays, which very effectively finance and collaborate with the racist Republic of South Africa.[22]

In addition to knocking the position of the Caribbean governments, the SALC led a demonstration outside the British High Commission whilst the test match was being played in Barbados. Michael Cummins, the chairman of SALC, stated:

Yesterday's demonstrations were to show how strongly the organization felt about the issue and the behavior of Caribbean governments. . . . The governments of Antigua, Barbados, Jamaica and Montserrat, at their meeting here two weeks ago had given Britain the green light to continue to breach Gleneagles as it has done in the past.[23]

The SALC was dissatisfied with the response of the Barbadian government when it discovered that a number of top English cricketers were going on a rebel tour of South Africa. It felt that this subdued response stemmed from the government's uncritical acceptance of U.S. foreign policy in relation to South Africa. However, they commended the government for stating that these players would not be allowed to play cricket in Barbados.[24] SALC stated:

South African sporting authorities clearly need international sports people to come to South Africa so that they can show the world South Africa still has friends to play with and that all is well in sport in that country. We must throw a spanner in the works of this plan and continue to show that race separation, the deprivation of the human rights of the South African black, East Indian and colored peoples in all aspects of South African society, will not be tolerated by humanity.[25]

The SALC was stung when the movement learnt of the impending tour to South Africa by a number of West Indian cricketers. This development represented a slap in the face to them and Africans worldwide who were engaged in the anti-apartheid struggle. The anti-apartheid struggle represented one of the strongest adhesives of the Pan-African project- all Africans were in agreement that this system must be destroyed. Therefore, to hear that a group of black West Indians who would have to accept the title of honorary whites in order to play in South Africa was a bitter pill for SALC to swallow. This development presented a challenge to the principle of isolating apartheid and reversing the successes scored by 'those who have already turned their backs on South African blood-drenched bribe money.' However, the SALC resolved that:

> We must in unity truly mobilize for sanctions against South Africa. We must in unity raise the campaign for the release of all political prisoners to a higher level. We must in unity ensure that we stop the flow of sports people and artistes to apartheid in South Africa.[26]

The United Nations Special Committee against Apartheid had recommended the strategy of isolating all sporting contacts with South Africa because it was seen as useful tactic in the anti-apartheid struggle. The Special Committee Against Apartheid at the United Nations, in its Introduction to the Second Register of Sports Contact, published in February 1982, called for an end to all contact with South Africa.

> The oppressed people of South Africa have called for a total boycott of sports exchanges with South Africa and have found a response from the great majority of government and sports bodies of the world. Those who prefer to abhor apartheid, and continue to collaborate with South Africa, must be exposed.[27]

At the anti-apartheid solidarity meeting, the SALC, the Caribbean Council of Churches (CCC), the West Indies Group of University Teachers (WIGUT), the Spiritual Baptist, the Catholic Church, the Movement for National Liberation (MONALI) and other organizations passed the following resolutions and submitted them to Prime Minister Tom Adams:

1. That the Barbadian government urgently inquire whether immigration and security regulations were breached to facilitate the departure of a number of prominent Barbadians who from reports were on their way to play in South Africa

in violation of the United Nations Resolutions against sports contact in that country.

2. That the Barbadian government moves to take the appropriate measure in the Customs Department in Barbados to make sure that no South African made goods are brought back into the island either on the said cricketers' person or through other means.

3. That the Barbadian government enforce the existing tax laws on the monies received by these cricketers from the South African authorities and that these said collected taxes be turned over to be used in such beneficial and meaningful work as that being carried out by such organizations as the World Council of Churches and the liberation movements themselves in Southern Africa to assist refugees fleeing from the horrors and hardship of racism and apartheid in South Africa and Namibia.

4. That the Barbados government support the plea of the SALC to the Barbados Cricket Association (BCA) that the players, who to all intents and purposes have gone to South Africa to play as members of a West Indies team, be banned from playing in Barbados club cricket for five years in addition to the already existing ban on them playing in future test matches for the West Indies.[28]

The SALC extended kudos to the West Indian players like Vivian Richards, Clive Lloyd, Joel Garner and Malcolm Marshall who refused to go to South Africa. According to the SALC, "these individuals have demonstrated that they are not only talented sportsmen but also responsible citizens of the Caribbean, who are sensitive to the sufferings of fellow human beings who are oppressed and exploited primarily because they are black." Moreover, their refusal to accept South African contracts will be remembered and appreciated as an important contribution to the struggle of the oppressed in South Africa. The SALC was confident that the "struggle led by the ANC in South Africa and SWAPO in Namibia must inevitably win."[29]

When the South Africa rugby team was allowed to play in New Zealand, the SALC was firm in its condemnation of the Muldoon regime. In a press release the SALC stated:

> The Muldoon Government in New Zealand was flagrantly violating the spirit and letter of the Gleneagles Accord, which prohibits sporting links by other countries with South Africa. SALC expresses its strong condemnation of the Muldoon regime which now stands exposed as a representative of minority opinion and a virulent opponent of basic human interests and the expressed will of the majority of the New Zealand people who are opposed to the tour.[30]

The SALC did an excellent job with its limited resources in raising the consciousness of Barbadians to the horrors of apartheid. They gave psychological and practical support (books to students from Namibia, clothes drive etc.) to the liberation movements in Southern Africa. By 1984, when the attention of the world focused on South Africa and the senselessness of apartheid, the SALC quietly receded into the background as other arms of civil society took up the mantle in sensitizing and condemning the apartheid system.

The Rastafarian Movement

The mid-1970s witnessed the growth and development of the Rastafarian movement in Barbados. According to Ronald Walters:

> One culturally powerful sector of the West Indian population that has exhibited a strong African consciousness and has thus been the carrier of a kind of Pan-Africanism is the Rastafarian.[31]

The Rastafarians have always identified very strongly with Africa, especially Ethiopia where Haile Selassie the Ethiopian monarch has been elevated to the status of a Messiah. Many of the brethren believed that they must repatriate either physically or psychologically to Ethiopia on the African continent, the land of their forefathers. The Rastafarians placed tremendous emphasis on black pride, by wearing their hair natural and challenging the centuries long racist view that suggested that nappy hair is not beautiful-indeed; many black women go to great lengths to have their hair straightened. The Rastafarians consistently promote the study of African history and African culture as well as the liberation of all black people. Moreover, the Rastafarians are anti-imperialist and anti-capitalist. Horace Campbell posits:

> The Rasta Movement in the Caribbean today is the foremost Pan-African and Pan-Caribbean movement in the area. Despite the idealist and oftimes metaphysical tenets of the movement, it is decidedly a section of the oppressed peoples and contains the history of their love for their homeland.[32]

The Rastafarian Movement has shown tremendous growth when many of major Pan-African organizations numbers have dwindled; and continues to be one of the leading torches of Pan-Africanism in Barbados.

The Marcus Garvey Hundredth Anniversary Committee

In 1987, on the centenary of Marcus Mosiah Garvey, a number of Pan-Africanists (Lloyd Jones, Claudette Drakes, Michael Cummins, Tony Cheeseman and David Commissiong) created the Marcus Garvey Hundredth Anniversary Committee. This organization sought to demonstrate that the ideas of Garvey were still relevant. Therefore, this body sought to raise the consciousness of Barbadians to the work of Garvey. The Marcus

Garvey Committee wanted Barbadians to reconnect to the African Continent spiritually, psychologically and psychically. To fulfill this objective, the movement held many discussions on Marcus Garvey and other great Pan- African figures on all the significant dates such as African Liberation Day, Namibia Day, SWAPO Day, and Ghana's Independence Day and on the birthdays of important figures like Amilcar Cabral. The members like the Pan-Africanists before them sought to de-educate the minds of the people from the negative images that were still prevalent about Africa due to the legacy of colonialism and the propagandizing efforts of the Western Media.[33]

The Marcus Garvey Committee lasted about three years before it exited the scene. Indeed, the limited objective of the movement straightjacketed its operations. After 1987, the movement was not as visible as before. Like the other Pan-African formations, its major successes can be seen as raising the consciousness and re-awakening Barbadians about their African heritage.

The Clement Payne Movement

David Commissiong, one of the major figures of the Marcus Garvey Committee, decided to create a Pan-African organization to occupy the vacuum created by the demise of the Marcus Garvey Committee. This led to the formation of the Clement Payne Cultural Centre/Clement Payne Movement in 1988. Many Pan-African veterans like David Commissiong, Martin Cadogan, Leroy Harewood, Trevor Prescod, David Denny, and John Howell became some of the leading figures of this organization.[34] Martin Cadogan must be given special mention as an important Pan-Africanist who ran as an independent in the 1986 General Elections. He stated: "as an independent, my philosophy will be based on Pan–Africanism, Nationalism and Nkrumahism. I believe in tapping the resources of the 35 million blacks in the United States and the 600 million in Africa." The premise of his platform was largely centered around the call on government to be committed to the liberation of Namibia; the liberation of South Africa—one man/one vote; to be committed to freeing Nelson Mandela; the renegotiation of the Gleneagles Agreement; the compulsory reading of Marcus Garvey in all secondary schools; embracing the Rastafarian element and teaching them to become useful citizens.[35] While Cadogan was unsuccessful in his quest at the polls he placed Pan-Africanism, Nelson Mandela and the South African struggle firmly on the national agenda.

Throughout their weekly meetings and discussions the Clement Payne Movement sought to keep the flames of Pan-Africanism burning. The Clement Payne Movement continued the program of the earlier Pan-Africanists and:

1. agitated for the recognition of the heroes of the 1937 disturbances (Clement Payne, Israel Lovell, Ulric Grant, Darnley Alleyne and Menzies Chase);
2. the removal of Lord Nelson from Broad Street;
3. the renaming of our streets from European heroes to black Barbadian heroes;
4. introduction of a system of community based government;
5. alien land holding legislation;
6. political union of the Eastern Caribbean,
7. the establishment of community based co-operatives;
8. the removal of the Queen from her position as Head of State of Barbados;
9. the development of people to people linkages between Barbados, Africa and the African Diaspora; and,
10. the teaching of Black Studies in schools.

The Clement Payne Movement also celebrated important occasions like July 26 and Emancipation Day.[36]

The leadership of the Clement Payne Movement believed that one of the major weaknesses they suffered from was a lack of state power. They felt drawn to the Nkrumah dictum, "seek ye first the political kingdom," in order to be able to transform society. Indeed, they saw this as the main weakness in the Pan-African formations

that preceded them.[37] Max Stafford was of the view that:

> Pan-African parties are the highest form of organization of African people in the struggle for national liberation. Of all organizations created by African people only a political party can give proper expression to the basic interest of the black underclass and lead it to victory.[38]

David Commissiong stated:

> My colleagues and myself . . . did consider forming a new political organization. However, we never thought of forming it out of the Clement Payne Labour Union. We have come to recognize that Barbadians have developed a suspicion of unions and political parties being closely linked in this era. . . . Those of us who see the need for a new political order do not have the luxury of a lot of time, so we recognize that with our limited human and financial resources that if we were to form a new party we would be looking at a substantially long period of development.[39]

To hasten this development the Clement Payne Movement joined the National Democratic Party (NDP). This development was not embraced by all of the Pan-Africanists, some of whom felt that that the Pan-Africanists should not align themselves with the NDP or any other political party. Indeed, given the experience of the Black Powerites who joined the BLP in the 1960s, these individuals were wary of alliances with political parties. However, David Commissiong was of the view that "the NDP is still in a fluid state and that it would be possible for persons like us to go into the party and make a substantial contribution in the formation of the party philosophy."[40] The Clement Payne Movement believed that it was quite possible to give the NDP a Pan-African orientation. However, from the inception of this alliance the perceptive Leroy Harewood posed the question in an article in the *Pulse* newspaper, "The Commissiong-Hayes alliance: Will it Work?"

According to Harewood:

> Philosophically, Mr. Commissiong and Dr. Haynes are as different as oil and water. Commissiong is a man with a formidable mission. He has taken it upon himself to try to accomplish what progressive young men like Bobby Clarke, Calvin Alleyne, Ossie Redman, Glenroy Straughn and others failed to achieve in the 1960s- the political, economic and cultural transformation of Barbadian society, where gross inequalities and glaring injustice would be removed from the fabric of Barbadian society.
>
> Mr. Commissiong is an idealist. He is an eternal optimist. . . . Mr. Commissiong finds it easy to associate and fight in the ranks of the under-privileged sector of Barbadian society.
>
> Dr. Richie Haynes on the other hand is a conservative . . . and slow to see the yawning chasm dividing various groups and classes in Barbados. Dr. Haynes sees the poverty and the misery of the poor, but these don't seem to cut into his consciousness with the same force as they cut into Commissiong's . . . while Mr. Commissiong constantly speaks in terms of black liberation, black redemption, and black dignity. Dr. Haynes hesitates to use what people called emotive language . . . Dr. Haynes speaks in sheer dollars and cents. Thus he remains cut off from the mainstream of Pan-Africanist thought, the cornerstone of Mr. Commissiong's philosophy.
>
> Dr. Haynes is a man grouping for a political and economic philosophy and a clear ethnic outlook. A serious student of Pan-Africanism, Mr. Commissiong's is sure that he has the correct political and economic philosophy as well as ethnic consciousness to grapple with the rock bottom issues that affect Barbadian society.
>
> . . . Can Dr. Haynes and his conservative supporters accept this change that Mr. Commissiong and his followers are trying to advocate in the NDP?[41]

David Commissiong and Trevor Prescod rose to the ranks of General Secretary and Vice President, while the other Pan-Africanists including Leroy Harewood, David Denny and Martin Cadogan failed to win any other positions on the NDP executive. Commissiong and Prescod contested the 1994 General Elections as members of the NDP and they were unsuccessful, however, the Pan-Africanist can take some credit for the overall performance of the NDP who did exceptionally well when compared with the last election in 1991 and in the constituencies where David Commissiong and Trevor Prescod competed.

The Clement Payne Movement failed in its quest to give the NDP a Pan-African face. However, it was evident that the NDP was speaking with a different voice than before their alliance with the Clement Payne Movement. In an address to the party, Haynes stated:

> We support and applaud the efforts of all who labor to build a better self-image among black people, who dedicate themselves to the cause of the poor, and who seek to elevate the consciousness of black people of their rich cultural heritage and put an end to false images of the past.
>
> Confrontation with and awareness of the truth of one's history is a necessary prerequisite for confidence in the present and the future. Both black and white Barbadians must unite and work together for a better future.[42]

In addition, the NDP manifesto spoke of placing greater emphasis on the scientific, technical and vocational aspects of education, as well as on the study of Barbadian history and society, and the history of African civilization. The party also spoke strongly about the need for a Barbadian Head of State.[43]

The Clement Payne Movement-NDP alliance suffered after Leroy Harewood challenged Richie Haynes for the presidency of the NDP. Peter Morgan felt that Leroy Harewood would gain his place in the political history of Barbados whether he won or lost, because "with the possible exception of Sir Grantley Adams at the formation of the BLP, there has never been a democratically elected political leader." Harewod stated that the reason he challenged Richie Haynes was because of his weak and vacillating leadership of the party.

> The leadership of the NDP is defective . . . because the leader is trying to make another DLP. He doesn't want any real, fundamental changes- he wants to model himself as a Barrow . . . and this is his fundamental mistake. So he's trying to go along the same elitist road hostile to people who dare to challenge his leadership . . .
>
> I am not concerned about what people called the expansion of education; I'm concerned with the quality of the education. You certainly have secondary schools, you have a lot of primary schools but what are they teaching? How do black people see themselves in relation to other people?
>
> What programs are in place to ensure that black people can hold their heads high and go places? That Blacks can control the commanding heights of their economy? . . . And you will notice that no politician in Barbados, and certainly (not) in the Black Diaspora, have addressed this problem. But nobody has ever addressed this mental sickness of Black people. A good example is what is happening at Thickets, Three Houses, Montcrieffe, in St. Phillip and Guinea Plantation in St. John. Recently we were told that these plantations have decided to go out of production because they don't have enough money to pay the people, Well, the workers would have seized those plantations as simple as that. . . . The land belongs to the people. . . . They are the workers; they have always been. These are the people who worked the plantation for years. Their fore parents were the slaves on the plantations and now they are the new slaves on the plantation. When I see

a white man or white woman on a plantation with a hoe
on a plantation, I would say that we have moved away
from slavery. Until that day comes we are still slaves. And
you can start by controlling a political party . . . as the
cutting edge for genuine advancement of the people. And
it is against this background, therefore, that I see myself as
becoming a leader of a political party, to use it as a cutting
edge to bring about the type of deep-seated transformation
that is necessary in Barbadian society.[44]

Harewood's colleagues David Denny and Martin Cadogan ran
for Vice President and General Secretary and were defeated. The
political fallout from this election was great, with both Harewood
and David Denny parting with the party with some degree of
bitterness. According to Harewood 'never before in my forty years
of association with various associations have I ever witnessed such
a deliberate attempt to silence non-executive members of a political
party.' Some of the members of the Clement Payne Movement left
and joined the BLP, with Trevor Prescod winning a seat on a BLP
ticket in 1999. However, some of the ideas of the Clement Payne
Movement were accepted by the NDP. For example the NDP's
manifesto spoke of teaching the history of Barbadian and African
civilization.[45]

The Clement Payne Movement can take some of the credit
for Clement Payne to be recognized as a national hero and the
attendant July 26, as a national day of significance. They can also
take some of the credit for Emancipation Day to be recognized
as a national holiday. The movement is still actively involved in
the Pan-African struggle although the movement has lost some
of its original members who for various reasons are no longer
active because of ideological splintering, (for example the African
Reparations group were once members of the Clement Payne
movement) as well as battle fatigue.

The Pan-African Movement of Barbados

In 1990, Naiwu Osahon, the Nigerian Pan-Africanist, issued the Call for Africans to organize themselves into Pan-African organizations. Throughout Global Africa many Pan-Africanists believed that the time was ripe to convene a 7th Pan-Africanist Congress:

> There is a widespread feeling among thoughtful members of the African race, of a need to revive the series of Pan-African Congresses. . . . The main objective of the 7th Pan-African congress . . . is to closely examine the problems of the Pan-African world, with a view of charting a strategy for our advancement in the 21st century.
>
> Today, some 400 years since our slavery began, ninety years into the Pan-African movement: thirty years after independence, sixteen years after the last congress, blacks all over the world constitute the dregs of society in which they live. We remain the poorest, most neglected, most abused of humanity and yet the most helpless because of our inability to work as one.
>
> Our problems today are multi-dimensional with both internal and external cause. . . . We have won tribal but not global African nationalism. Our mushroom hamlets have won flag independence but none of us have won the freedom to have a say in our destiny. And that is what Pan-Africanism should be about now, the freedom to direct our own affairs. An all out offensive against our problems is now called for and we need an all-embracing institution to spearhead the global assault on our behalf.[46]

Out of these Pan-African formations, representatives would be chosen to participate in this historic gathering. Many Pan-Africanists including Bobby Clarke, David Commissiong, George Belle, Kofi Akobi, Ricky Parris, David Denny, Viola Davis, Hilary

Beckles, Joy Workman and others heeded the "Call" and created the Pan-African Movement of Barbados. The veteran Pan-Africanist Bobby Clarke became the chairman of the Pan-African Movement of Barbados (PAMOB). The objectives of this organization were:

1. To act as a Coordinator and facilitator of Pan-Africanist work in Barbados;
2. To prepare for the representation and participation of Barbados in future International Pan-African Congresses;
3. To work towards the removal from the Barbadian polity, economy and society, all remaining hindrances to the advancement of African people;
4. To promote a calendar of activities to commemorate events of significance to African people;
5. To cooperate with all who seek to realize the ultimate goal of the unification of Africa and its people on the continent in the Caribbean and the Diaspora;
6. To work towards the progress and development of all African peoples;
7. To do other acts as are incidental or conducive to the attainment of the foregoing objectives.[47]

The overriding political objective was to work for the total liberation of the African continent and the Diaspora from the scourges of colonialism, neo-colonialism and imperialism. PAMOB launched an educational campaign to inform and educate the masses of Barbadians about its philosophy and programmes. The organization started a newspaper called the *New Vision* edited by Leroy Harewood, the former editor of the *Black Star* newspaper. The New Vision was expected to be the voice of Pan-Africanism in the Caribbean, "which would enlighten our people about their heritage, past culture, past strengths, past accomplishments and chart the path with a new vision."[48] Olutoye Walrond felt that:

The launching of *New Vision* by the Pan-African Movement of Barbados is a development fraught with positive implications for the African population of Barbados. In a country served by two conservative newspapers, each one rivaling the other in the promotion of minority interests, the appearance of the New Vision can only spell good for the enlightenment of the black masses of this country.

The work of the organization is quite clearly cut out; and the appearance of *New Vision* is perhaps a good way to begin. For in a post slavery society where there's an annual festival celebrating the arrival of the first slave masters and the first slaves in chains, there's obviously a monumental need for popular education and enlightenment.

In a society, which has embraced all the values, systems, allegiances—even dress—of its colonial oppressors, there's obviously a great task for the *New Vision* to perform. Where a black society which calls itself independent still finds it desirable to have as it head of state a mere foreigner, four thousand miles away, who clearly has no interest in our development, there's need for a new vision.[49]

Harewood, in the first editorial of the New Vision, was of the view that the black working class throughout the world has the right to affirm its full human rights. These rights are the right to decent housing, to proper medical care, to meaningful education. Harewood mentioned that these rights would be seriously compromised by the IMF/World Bank structural adjustment policies in Barbados and other countries. The PAMOB totally rejected the myth that was being propagated by the ruling class and their IMF masters during the austerity period of the early nineties, namely that all sectors of the Barbadian society were equally to blame for the foreign exchange shortage confronting the country. Indeed, PAMOB pointed out that the economic crisis was caused by the high consumption oriented life styles and business practices, certainly it was not caused by the working class, since the majority of their numbers existed on very meager resources in deprived housing conditions, with many of them barely able to eke out an existence. Furthermore, it was highly immoral to suggest that the burden of any structural adjustment must be borne by this class.[50] PAMOB consistently pointed out the dangers of entering into structural adjustment programs by showing how these programs impacted negatively on working people and the governance of the country (a form of re-colonization).

After Barbados missed the opportunity to bring Oliver Tambo (leader of the African National Congress) to Barbados, the PAMOB of Barbados wrote a letter inviting Nelson Mandela to visit Barbados, this letter read:

> Dear Brother,
> The Pan-African Movement of Barbados extends to Bro. Nelson Mandela Vice President of the African Nationalist Congress an Invitation on behalf of all African peoples of Barbados to visit us during your Caribbean and Latin America tour in August 1991. Africa holds a special place to Barbados and its people, as we were the first stop in the passage of our forefathers.
>   Your courage has given all African people the hope that one day we shall all be united as one.
>   We request your confirmation on this matter as soon as possible.
>   Together
>   Bobby Clarke.[51]

The membership of PAMOB enthusiastically sought to build and develop the organization. Indeed, the newsletter of the international Pan-African coordinating committee rated PAMOB as the number one branch worldwide, a model for other Pan-African bodies to follow, PAMOB got this rating because it:

1. Held a fortnightly radio program called "Africa must Unite;"
2. Started a monthly newspaper called the New Vision;
3. Held fund-raising programs for the relief of the famine in Africa;
4. Staged a preparatory Caribbean Conference of Pan-African

organizations in 1991 (at this conference the following topics were discussed and resolutions were passed on Grass Roots involvement in building the 7th PAC and developing alternatives to the IMF and World Bank, Communications, Technology & Culture as for African Self Determination & Collective Self Reliance, Repatriation, Reparations, Lessons from the Grenadian and Ethiopian Revolutions, Pan-African Skills Bank on Science & Technology, Pan-Africanism and the New World Order);

5.   Started an anti-poverty program in Barbados;
6.   Established an agricultural co-operative and a Pan-African trading Company.[52]

Many of these ambitious programs did not meet with the success hoped for. Nevertheless, these programs still form part of the Pan-African project, although they suffered from a critical shortage of capital. Bobby Clarke and David Commissiong took part in the 7th Pan-African Congress in Uganda in 1994.

The hosting of the Caribbean conference of Pan-African organizations by PAMOB was a very historic development within the Pan-African sphere. At this conference seven delegations took part namely the African Friendship Association of Dominica, which was headed by Irvine Knight; the Pan-African Movement of St. Lucia, headed by Michael McCombie; the All African Peoples Revolutionary Party of St. Croix, headed by Moreni Hunt; the Universal African Improvement Association of Trinidad and Tobago, headed by Delores Omisaru Alexander; the Seventh Pan-African Congress Committee of Trinidad and Tobago, headed by Felipe Noguera; and the Pan-African Movement of Barbados, headed by Bobby Clarke. The delegates arrived at four major decisions: (i) the transformation of the PAMOB's Executive Committee to serve as regional secretariat for the Caribbean area; (ii) the development of the Barbadian New Vision into a regional journal, (iii) the setting up of a permanent committee on science and technology which will be working out of Guyana, with a view of conceptualizing a Pan-Africanist philosophy and program of science and industrial development; (iv) the establishment of a region-wide commercial enterprise to carry out the production and distribution of Pan-Africanist cultural paraphernalia.[53]

The Barbadian conference sought to reach a united position on several issues of fundamental importance to African peoples worldwide, such as the IMF assault on the Third World, the so-called New World Order, cultural and ideological imperialism, and the principles of unity for the 7th Pan-African Congress. The conference passed several resolutions such as: the removal of the United States trade embargo against Cuba, the commitment of the Pan-African Movement to a campaign against the forthcoming celebrations of the Columbus Myth in 1992, to make common cause with the United Nations Children Emergency Fund (UNICEF) and the Bretton Woods Reform Organization, in their efforts to reform the IMF and its policies towards Third World countries, to reorient the Pan-African Movement around a non-elitist, mass based, grass roots philosophy and programme, the positive role of the Caribbean Rastafarian movement as an integral part of the Pan-African struggle. Moreover, the conference endorsed the call for repatriation of Africans desirous of returning physically to their racial mother land, while at the same time the delegates affirmed the rights of all Africans to be paid reparations arising out of slavery. The conference acknowledged the heroism and solidarity of the Cuban leadership and people, especially in the Southern African revolutionary struggle.[54]

While many of the original warriors have retreated from PAMOB, the organization is still a viable Pan-African entity on the Barbadian landscape.

The Commission for Pan-African Affairs

In 1998, the Barbadian government created the Commission for Pan-African Affairs. This organization was headed by David Commissiong, the chairman of the Clement Payne Movement. The creation of this body was a significant departure from Pan-

Africanism in the past. Previously, Pan-African activity was
normally associated with left wing fringe groups and so-called
"madmen." This organization was also viewed with great suspicion
by some Pan-Africanists, who felt that this was one means by
which the BLP government was seeking to silence the voices of
the left. Many of the veteran Pan-Africanists remembered what
happened to important leaders of the Black Power Movement
who joined the BLP in the early 70s. At the official opening of this
body Prime Minister Owen Arthur stated:

> We are predominately a people of African origin; yet as a
> people, as a nation, we have built full-fledged economic,
> political and cultural relationships with people of every
> continent and every race except the African continent.
>   We have valued greatly, and will continue to value
> the relationships we have forged with the nations and
> people of the world. But I say to you, this therefore merely
> casts on us an overwhelming obligation to deal with the
> missing link in our affairs to build and value a profound
> relationship with all things African, at home and abroad.
>   The century just about to end has been often cited as
> the American century, in the sense that it saw the rise of
> the USA to be a great nation. Well, there has been a great
> reawakening in Africa, led and energized by the liberation
> of Southern Africa. And I confidently say to you that the
> next century, the 21st Century, may well come to be the
> African Century
>   It is for us of African origin to make it happen!
>   Our Pan-African Commission will therefore seek to
> reach out from our Caribbean island territory to re-develop
> the bonds with Africa and the African Diaspora that were
> so traumatically dislocated centuries ago.
>   It will proclaim and champion the cultural and political
> phenomenon known as Pan-Africanism and nurture the
> practical application of the concept that there is an objective
> commonality of interest and purpose between Africa,

Africans, and African descendants worldwide. It will play its part in the efforts to regenerate and unify Africa and to promote a feeling of unity among the people of African origin and other races.[55]

In an effort to carry out its objectives The Commission For Pan-African Affairs identified the following projects as priorities:

1. The establishment of an international "think thank" comprising a number of the best and most creative minds of the Pan-African world;
2. The development of student exchange programs with African countries and black educational institutions of the Diaspora;
3. The formulation of an African studies curriculum for Caribbean schools;
4. The establishment of direct airline linkages between the Caribbean and the continent of Africa;
5. The facilitation of contacts between Barbadian private and public sector institutions and their counterparts in Africa and the Diaspora;
6. The organized exchange of news, films, music and general information within the Pan-African world;
7. The facilitation of exchange visits by the musicians, dancers, literary artists, sports people, visual artists and crafts-people of Africa and the Diaspora;
8. The development of trade and tourism linkages with the nations and population groups of Africa and the Diaspora;
9. The elaboration of a program to facilitate the employment of skilled Barbadian technicians and professionals on the African continent;
10. The development of a broad based Pan-African campaign for the payment of reparations to the nations and peoples of Africa and the Diaspora;
11. The fostering of a broad based Pan-African and Caribbean lobby in the countries of North America and Europe;
12. The development of a program to facilitate Diaspora Africans

interested in returning to Africa.[56]

The Commission for Pan-African Affairs has brought a number of outstanding Pan-Africanists to lecture to Barbadian audiences. Moreover, the Commission has sponsored the African Century Symposium where scholars and activists met and discussed the condition of the black world and what must be done to lift it from its present condition. This author believes it is too early to carry out a useful examination of the work of the Commission in realizing its ambitious objectives, and to what extent, if any, has taken Pan-Africanism in Barbados forward or to what extent it has retarded or discredited the work of the Pan-African formations.

Conclusion

So the return to the source is of no historical importance unless it brings not only real involvement in the struggle for independence, but also complete and absolute identification with the hopes of the masses of people, who contest not only the foreign culture but also foreign domination as a whole. Otherwise the return to the source is nothing more than an attempt to find short-term benefits–knowingly or unknowingly, a kind of political opportunism.
Amilcar Cabral, *The Return To the Source*

The Pan-African formations that have been the basis of this study have all fought a valiant fight in the protracted struggle against race and class domination, colonialism, neo-colonialism, imperialism, black-disenfranchisement, apartheid and euro-centrism. These groupings also fought to bring about black unity as a necessary pre-requisite to bring about black dignity and fight against all the economic, social and political disabilities facing the black Barbadian masses. In addition, these Pan-Africanists knew no boundaries when Black people worldwide were being threatened as seen in the Italian invasion of Ethiopia, the struggle against apartheid, and the civil rights struggle in the United States of America. The Pan-African bodies offered tremendous support in the above battles to prevent the savaging of their brothers and sisters worldwide in the struggle for dignity and justice.

These Pan-African movements/formations battled against extreme odds in a very reactionary political order in the quest for the betterment of the African masses. Many of the members suffered financially, were discriminated against, vilified and classified as being madmen who were harassed by the police authorities. However, history has vindicated these Pan-Africanists who in many cases were the conscience of the people in leading the struggle against societal injustices. They can feel proud of their work in trying to educate the black masses of their proud and glorious past and challenging the myths and fairy tales propagated about the black race.

The present conjuncture of rabid neo-liberalism and triumphant capitalism will present tremendous challenges to Pan-Africanism in Barbados and Pan-Africanism world wide in the twenty first century. Therefore, the Pan-African formations that presently exist must seek to find a new vibrant language that speaks to the issues that confront the masses. This language will allow these bodies to engage in a process of mass mobilization, whereby more women and youth will be attracted to the fold. Any movement that is devoid of women and youth will lack the political dynamism and critical perspectives that will better inform and sharpen the analysis of these bodies on any issue. Thus greater emphasis must be placed on attracting the youth and women into their folds.

Historically, the Pan-Formations while being said to be democratic have been led by charismatic leaders, where the personality of the leader has overshadowed the whole movement; when the leaders exited the scene these movements have suffered gravely. Therefore the Pan-African formations need selfless enlightened leadership that have integrity, dedication, magnanimity, humility, openness and creativity in order to engage the forces of reaction and function effectively in the prevailing climate. Greater emphasis must be placed on building strong mass based Pan-African organizations and empowering the African masses so as to enable them to transform their societies. The issues of democracy, transparency and accountability must become the bedrock of Pan-Africanism.

At this juncture there is a definite need for some organ to disseminate the views of the Pan-Africanists. The Pan-Africanists must have some medium, whether a web site, newspaper, or journal. The forces of reaction have their own medium, as well as access to the popular medium to counteract the progressive views of the Pan-Africanists and win followers into their camps.

Pan-African bodies need its 'think tanks' and strong vibrant research arms. Indeed, there is a crying need for more empiricism and critical analysis coming from the Pan-Africanists on many critical issues. We have reached the stage where less emphasis should be placed on anecdotal claims and myth making because it raises serious questions about the credibility of our Pan-African organization. The reactionary elements have a large pool of resource persons and institutions that give their cause some degree of 'credibility' in the battle for the minds of the people.

At the level of social theory the Pan-Africanists must bear in mind that capitalism has been the enemy of the masses of black people. Therefore, the Pan-African formations must critique the various initiatives undertaken by the capitalist project to further disadvantage the masses of black workers all over the world. The Pan-African bodies of the past century have laid the foundation for Pan-Africanism in the new century.

Appendix

This writer carried out a number of interviews with some of the leading Pan-Africanist figures in Barbados, in order to get a better understanding of the inner workings of various Pan-African groupings. These interviews were very informative and enlightening; they clarified many issues, provided useful commentaries and contributed immensely towards an understanding of, and an appreciation for, the work of the Pan-African formations operating in Barbados, once considered a bastion of conservatism. These Pan-Africanists were able to help the author to understand the struggles, the climate, financial constraints, sacrifices, harassments, ideological tensions, and even some of the personalities and personality clashes that were a feature of these organizations. This author has selected and edited four interviews with four leading Pan-African activists in Barbados.

Interview with Kofi Akobi (Bridgetown, Barbados, September 12, 1998)

Kofi Akobi is the current Chairman of the Pan-African Movement of Barbados. He was a member of Yoruba (Youth Rural and Urban of Barbados) and was heavily involved in the activities of Black Night. He was one of the leading Black Powerites in the late sixties, before he was co-opted by the Barbados Labour Party, along with

Elombe Mottley the leading spokesmen on Black Power in Barbados.

Worrell: Brother Kofi can you tell me about Black Night, Yoruba and your early involvement in Pan-Africanism.

Akobi: We were part of a group Known as Black Night, which used to meet on Baxter's Road during the late sixties, the radical musicians and poets were able to intermingle and exchange ideas on politics, law and issues of independence. Black Night was poetry and music—El Verno Del Congo, Vere Gibson, Vere Millar, Boo Rudder, Ernie Small and Shilling. Those people were expressing the Barbadian culture in Bajan terms rather than expressing English culture in English terms.

Yoruba meant Youth Rural and Urban of Barbados. Many people don't even know this, because Yoruba was the name of an ethnic group in Nigerian, people assumed that was it. The importance of the work done by Yoruba cannot be over emphasized; it was there that Barbadians were exposed to John Henrik Clarke, the Holder Brothers, Ed Smith and Aretha Franklin. Yoruba was the brain child and baby of Elombe Mottley. We were attempting to do a play, "Cain Mangoes," by a Cuban playwright that was very relevant to Black people in the Caribbean. "Cain Mangoes" would be breaking new ground, it was a play set outside the Eastern Caribbean, but still within the Caribbean. A dispute arose as to who should direct the play, this led to the breaking up of the Barbados Theatre Workshop since the Theatre Workshop could not withstand the loss of some of the more talented persons within the organization.

Yoruba played an important part in expressing black consciousness—the works of Angela Davis and Eldridge Cleaver were studied, persons were exposed to information on Africa, and shoulders were rubbed with radical personalities from within the Caribbean, Pan-Africanists, politicians and trade unionists.

Worrell: Was there a connection between Black Night and the Embryonic Black power movement?

Akobi: The Black Power Movement in Barbados emerged on many fronts. The *Black Star* newspaper was tremendous—Glenroy Straugh, Ossie Redman, Calvin Alleyne, Bobby Clarke, Leroy Harewood, Veronica Harewood, and John Connell brought a new awareness and a new consciousness to the Barbadian landscape. Rameses Caddle also played an important role in raising the consciousness of the average Barbadian. *Black Star* and Caddle must be commended for contributing to the heightened consciousness of Barbadians.

Race became an issue in Barbados like never before, because the people became exposed to the radical writings of individuals like Frantz Fanon. At this time corporate Barbados was frightened because of what was happening in Barbados. They had never seen Black people saying the things that were now being said. We were dealing with a time when Black was a bad word, nobody said Black; people would say Negro or color. They held a meeting and we put our complaints to the system and they made some concessions to make the situation less volatile. However, a fundamental issue like land was never dealt with. Most of the girls that worked in the Banks were White or of a certain complexion. Many Blacks who are in managerial positions today owed their advancement to what was happening during this period. However, with hindsight our major shortcoming was not making the land a major issue. At that time White people in Barbados had started to run from Barbados. Cracks started to develop within the plantocracy. That was the perfect opportunity to divide up the plantations among the people who worked on the plantations. What happened instead was the lawyers, politicians and professionals saw the opportunity to take over from the White people; they wanted their own four and ten acre lots.

Worrell: How did you get involved with the Barbados Labour Party?

Akobi: Conditions in Barbados had started to get less than favorable for the average person, discontentment was becoming very real. The Barbados Labor Party chose that opportunity to seek an alliance with some elements of the Black Power movement. Elombe and myself joined the party under the impression that the Barbados Labor Party was going to incorporate some elements of the Black Power program into their program. I held the position of Assistant General Secretary and the editor of the *Beacon* for a number of issues during the 1970s. We felt that we could build a power base within the party. The Barbados Labor Party did not incorporate any of our ideas in their 1970 manifesto. I subsequently resigned from the party.

Worrell: What about your involvement with the Pan-African Movement of Barbados.

Akobi: I was the Chairman of the Pan-African Movement of Barbados for the last three years and was a member of the executive for the last eight years. Bobby Clarke was the first Chairman, David Denny was the first secretary. The Pan-African Movement of Barbados was an attempt by the progressives to redress the imbalances. I strongly believe that the Pan-African Movement of Barbados should be non-partisan and stay clear of both political parties in Barbados. The best thing the movement can do is to maintain a rigid neutral position. By that, I mean to have an objective and work for its realization.

Interview with Michael Cummins (Bridgetown, Barbados, August 31, 1998)

Michael Cummins was the long-serving Chairman of the Southern African Liberation Committee (SALC). He is still involved in Pan-African struggle as a member of the Pan-African Movement of Barbados.

Worrell: Michael how did you became involved with the Southern Africa Liberation Committee?

Cummins: The first political organization I became a member of was Youth Organization for Revolutionary Change in 1974. The main activities were annual African Liberation Day marches in Queens Park, public rallies, and other forums held at Yoruba yard. I remember a rally that was addressed by Joseph Dube, the representative of the Patriotic Front of Zimbabwe, who was based in Cuba; he spoke about the anti-apartheid movement. A meeting was held on Tuesday, September 15, 1977, at the home of Elombe Mottley. At this meeting/get together Rosie Douglas, Elombe Mottley, Ricky Parris, and Brother Dube agreed that there was a need for an organization to lend support to the struggle against apartheid in South Africa and the struggle in Southern Africa. Out of this informal gathering the seeds of the Southern African Liberation Committee were sown. A letter was drafted and sent to sixty-five organizations and individuals who were identified as already having an interest in this type of activity or we thought should be involved. Some of these organizations were the Barbados Workers Union, the Barbados Union of Teachers, Churches, and persons who had spoken about the problems facing black people in South Africa. By this time we had started to refer to ourselves as the Southern African Co-ordinating Committee. On December 3, 1977, we held our first executive meeting that was when the Southern African Liberation Committee was formed.

Some of the organizations we thought would be in the forefront of this initiative particularly the trade unions gave us a cold response. However, the response was generally good, a lot of persons wanted to find out what the organization was doing and others gave tactical support, while not being there at our meetings.

Worrell: At that juncture were the members very much in tune with the developments taking place in Southern Africa?

Cummins: At the time we had very strong sentiments and understood the need for Black people in Barbados and the Black Diaspora to be concerned, involved, and carry out work in solidarity with those in Southern Africa. But we needed more information and the experience that would come about with greater involvement.

Worrell: Who were some of the members of the first executive?

Cummins: Canon Sehon Goodridge was the first Chairman, Brother Sholar Holawan, a Nigerian attached to Yoruba House, was the cultural officer, Father Harcourt Blackett was the educational officer, Elombe Mottley was the public relations person, and Michael Cummings was the Vice Chairman. However, I was disappointed that many of the people did not see the struggle against apartheid as a moral struggle. It was fundamental to morality, justice, goodness, fairness, and equality. The church which is supposed to be leading a moral struggle and have a great deal of credibility was well placed to speak out against this injustice. Canon Goodridge and Father Blackett became very isolated even within the church. Canon Goodridge was under a fair deal of pressure especially when he spoke about the operations of Barclays Bank and others who were operating in Barbados, and had firms in South Africa or carried out business with companies in South Africa. Canon Goodridge went away on a sabbatical and he was later stationed elsewhere, he led the Southern African Liberation Committee for about one year.

Worrell: Was the Southern African Liberation Committee only concerned with the struggle in Southern Africa? What about Barbados?

Cummins: I was very conscious and careful that the Southern African Liberation Committee would stick to its portfolio and concentrate on the problems facing Southern Africa. However, there were some local issues that were connected to the issues in South Africa. The Barrow Democratic Labour Party administration was quite lapsed in allowing a foreign company of the magnitude of High Altitude Research Project (HARP) to come into the country with so many concessions that they evolved into a Space Research Program. When the Tom Adams administration was confronted with the information the response was slow, the government did not immediately closed down Space Research Corporation, it was not given an ultimatum, and no clear condemnation of the organization was given by the government. Joshua Nkomo one of the co-leaders of the Zimbabwean Patriotic Front accused the Space Research Corporation of selling artillery shells and technology to South Africa; the Barbados government did not listened to the Patriotic Front. They allowed the organization to continue its operation until its contract expired. Dr. Bull was prosecuted in North America and imprisoned for six months but none of the functionaries here in Barbados were properly investigated, if investigated at all. After hearing Nkomo's revelation we launched an aggressive campaign against Space Research Corporation and sought to keep the matter in front of the public. A large part of the campaign against SRC was also waged in Antigua by Tim Hector's Antigua Afro-Caribbean Liberation Movement (ACLM). We cooperated fairly closely with the ACLM especially on this issue.

Worrell: The Southern African Liberation Committee's position on the English cricketers who played cricket in South Africa seemed fairly tamed? What was the impact of the West Indian cricketers going to apartheid South Africa on the Southern African Liberation Committee?

Cummins: Let us be clear, the Bionic Manshop was importing shirts from South Africa. Custom officials found the shirts and confiscated them. At the time we felt that this was an area of greater priority so that we organized demonstrations outside the store. We also organized a demonstration against Graham Gooch coming to Barbados. Southern African Liberation Committee also took a strong position on the Robin Jackman Affair and we felt that Guyana's position should be supported. The Caribbean governments were not unanimous in their condemnation of the apartheid struggle. Southern African Liberation Committee felt that the Caribbean should be united against the apartheid system. The Guyanese government was very strong on this issue but the majority of Caribbean governments were weak on the anti-apartheid issue. When the Robin Jackman dispute arose we met the touring English cricket team at the airport with a demonstration. It was quite significant that the press did not approach anyone from Southern African Liberation Committee for the reasons we were engaged in this protest.

Lawrence Rowe rebel tour impacted very heavily on the consciousness of the Caribbean. It threw the anti-apartheid struggle in the Caribbean into a state of confusion. Students in South Africa wanted to know how come they invited Black West Indian cricketers to play cricket but would not encourage Black South Africans to play.

Worrell: What were some of your major achievements?

Cummins: They are many small things: working and hosting students from South Africa and Namibia who came here to study, working with them to make them feel at home. I have no doubt that we contributed towards the raising of public consciousness on the horrors of the apartheid system in South Africa. It was only after the Soweto uprising that the problem became better understood, not only in Barbados but also worldwide. We attended conferences held by the United Nations in Costa Rica and Venezuela.

Worrell: What about frustrations?

Cummins: The duplicity of the government. We were heartened when Henry Forde the Minister of Foreign Affairs came out and supported the Southern African Liberation Committee on its launch. However, we began to encounter problems, too much sensitivity and not enough cooperation. When the young democrats distributed over one thousand shirts, we could not get the shirts to the refugees of apartheid. There were breaches of the trade embargo with South Africa; companies that transgressed were only given a slap on the wrist. The government was claiming to be anti-apartheid but its action was not very firm and decisive in this regard.

Interview with Lloyd Jones (Bridgetown, Barbados, September 3, 1998)

Lloyd Jones is a committed Garveyite. He was one of the main individuals behind the Marcus Garvey Hundredth Anniversary Committee. Lloyd Jones is a member of the Pan-African Movement of Barbados.

Worrell: Can you shed some light on the idea behind the Marcus Garvey Committee?

Jones: The year 1987 was the Hundredth Anniversary of the Birth of Marcus Mosiah Garvey. All those individuals that he touched worldwide decided to put on something to honor him. Therefore we in Barbados started the Hundredth Anniversary Committee. We got started on March 6, the thirtieth anniversary of Ghana's independence, since Kwame Nkrumah was the standard bearer of Garvey and sought to bring about the organic unification of Africa with a Union Government. We had a big fanfare in Queens Park on August 17, Garvey's birthday. Ironically, Barbados with a high population of persons of African ancestry had projected Africa as the continent of darkness. This happened because of the dragnet of European education particularly in the primary schools. What we attempted to do was to help raise some consciousness about Africa. For example on Namibia Day, August 26, we kept a meeting; our program was mainly educational. The problem was to sustain the educational program around Africa when you had CNN and CBC showing all the negative images of Africa, starvation in Sudan and fighting in Sierra Leone. Also on an island where insularity has been a big problem, people were asking what was the relevance of a Jamaican national hero to Barbadians? They could not understand the vision of Marcus Garvey in unifying Blacks around the world. They still saw themselves as Bajans, although one has a Caricom and the OECS, we can't seem to get past the insularity problem.

Worrell: Was the Marcus Garvey Committee active in providing information on Africa?

Jones: You have to de-educate the Anglican Church and its primary education. The Anglican Church was a tool of colonialism and sought to create a more faithful British citizen. This was an almost impossible task for a committee of twenty five persons. We did not have the skills of Marcus Garvey who was a wonderful publicist as manifested in the *Negro World* and the *Black Man*.

We were into the guts, the core of Marcus Garvey. Even within our organization they were always these ongoing debates, because some people were just interested in wearing African attire, but could not deal with the philosophical Africa for the Africans, those at home and abroad.

Worrell: Did you seek to create a mass movement?

Jones: That would have been our secondary objective; our strategy to move the people forward was to detoxify them. We wanted Barbadians to reconnect to an African civilization. We have nothing to be ashamed of; all we have to do is to shake off the last five hundred year history. We were trying to jolt the Barbadian status quo, who lacked the information about Africa, and who wanted to be associated with the colonial past and the British and American society. We wanted to do all of this with no organ, no access to radio, television, or the press.

Interview with David Commissiong (Bridgetown, Barbados, September 15, 1998)

David Commissiong is the Director of the Commission for Pan-African Affairs, an organization created by the Barbados government. He is the Chairman of the Clement Payne Movement, the leading Pan-Africanist organization in Barbados. David Commissiong was also a member of the Marcus Garvey Hundredth Anniversary Committee and a former General Secretary of the Pan-African Movement of Barbados. He was also a Senator and was one of the two Barbadian representatives at the seventh Pan-African Congress (1994) in Uganda.

Worrell: How did you get involved in Pan-Africanism?

Commissiong: My involvement stems from an invitation by Lloyd Jones to form a Committee to celebrate the Centenary of Marcus Garvey. We met and formed the Marcus Garvey Committee, this organization did a tremendous amount of work. The organization ran out of steam and I had an idea of forming a more permanent organization, which of course was the Clement Payne Cultural Centre. I invited the persons who were involved in the Marcus Garvey Committee to take the plunge to acquire a building for a more permanent organization—that was around 1988/1989; the invitation was not taken up. I forged ahead and that was how the Clement Payne Cultural Centre was born.

Worrell: Why Clement Payne?

Commissiong: When the centre was born it did not have a name, it was just called the Reed Street Centre. I took some time looking for an appropriate name (one that would be called after a black working class hero) that would give the centre its identity; that was why the name Clement Payne was chosen. The 1937 heroes were tragically swept under the carpet and I felt that something had to be done to bring this to the attention of the public. At the launching of the Clement Payne Centre, an attempt was made to pull back the veteran Pan-African fighters, Leroy Harewood, Calvin Alleyne, Glenroy Straugh, Bobby Clarke, John Connell, and George Belle. We were cognizant that we were building on the foundations that had been laid by those elders and working class activist.

Worrell: What was your level of involvement with the Pan-African Movement of Barbados?

Commissiong: I was a founding member of Pan-African Movement of Barbados. Many of the Pan-African organizations that were born after 1989 had their genesis in the Clement Payne Cultural Centre. I held the post of the General Secretary of Pan-African Movement of Barbados; in the early days, many of the meetings were held right at the Clement Payne Cultural Centre. Nigeria sent out the Call to the entire Black World to organize Pan-African organizations with a view of holding the seventh Pan-African Congress. Ricky Parris, David Denny, Bobby Clarke, George Belle, Linden Lewis, Hilary Beckles, and some university students responded to the Call. The Pan-African Movement of Barbados was one of the most energetic branches; we were the first branch to have a constitution and to start a newspaper. The Barbadian branch became the spearhead of the Pan-African branches in the Caribbean and hosted a Caribbean Pan-African gathering.

Worrell: Why did you seek to form an alliance with the National Democratic Party?

Commissiong: By 1994 it had become clear to some of the members of the Clement Payne Centre that a greater effort must be made to grasp political power. We felt that serious Pan-Africanists must seek state power. Therefore, we could no longer afford to be involved in partisan politics. We thought about forming our own political party but that did not seem a likely proposition. We held meetings with Dr. Haynes' Party, our thinking was that we could worked with the National Democratic Party and give the organization a Pan-Africanist philosophy and locate ourselves within the formal political structures in Barbados.

Worrell: What was your moment of success?

Commissiong: I would say the decision by the government of Barbados to set up a Pan-African Commission. Barbados is the only Black Country that has set up such an organization whose mandate is to pursue a Pan-African mandate. The Commission provides us with an opportunity to pull the Pan-African Movement together using the resources of the state. The recognition of July 26 as a Day of National Significance, Emancipation Day as a national holiday, National Heroes Day and the recognition of Clement Payne, Bussa, and others as national heroes, are also areas of great success after several years of agitation and struggle.

Notes

Chapter 1

[1] See Neville Duncan, *Movements as Sub-cultures — A Preliminary Examination of Social and Political Protest in the Anglophone Caribbean*, 1983, 2.

[2] See Gary Rush and R. Serge Denisoff, *Social and Political Movements* (New York: Meredith Corporation 1971), 2.

[3] *ibid.*

[4] *ibid.*, 3.

[5] *ibid.*

[6] *ibid.*, 5.

[7] See Immanuel Geiss, *The Pan-African Movement*, trans. by Anna Keep (London: Methuen 1974), 3.

[8] *ibid.*

[9] See Colin Legum, *Pan-Africanism: A short Political Guide* (London: Pall Mall Press 1962), 14.

[10] *ibid.*

[11] See W. Ofuatey-Kodjoe's definition in Ronald Walters, *Pan-Africanism in the African Diaspora: An Analysis of Modern Afro-Centric Political Movements* (Detroit: Wayne State University 1993), 48.

[12] P. Olisuwuche Esedebe, *Pan-Africanism* (Washington: Harvard University Press 1983), 3.

[13] Tony Martin, *The Pan-African Connection, from Slavery to Garvey and Beyond* (Massachusetts: The Majority Press 1984), VII.

[14] See Judith Stein, *The World of Marcus Garvey: Race and Class in Modern Society* (Louisiana: Louisiana State University Press 1986), 7.

[15] See Horace Campbell, "Pan-Africanism in the Twenty-first Century," in *Pan-Africanism: Politics, Economy and Social Change in the Twenty- First*

Century, Tajudeen Abdul- Raheem, eds. (New York: New York University Press 1996), 219.

[16] Rodney Worrell, *Pan-Africanism In the New Global Conjuncture. Has the Internationalization of Capital Rendered this Concept Irrelevant?* M.Phil Thesis. (University of the West Indies, Cave Hill, 1999): 13; and Rodney Worrell, "Pan-Africanism in Barbados," in Glenford Howe & Don Marshall, *The Empowering Impulse: The Nationalist Tradition in Barbados* (Kingston: University of the West Indies Press).

[17] See Peter Gutkind and Immanuel Wallerstein, *The Political Economy of Contemporary Africa* (California: Sage Publications, 1976), 33; and Immanuel Wallerstein, *The Capitalist World Economy* (London: Cambridge University Press, 1979), 27-41.

[18] Tony Martin, VII.

[19] See Tony Martin, "The Caribbean and Pan-Africanism," in *The African Caribbean Connection, Historical and Cultural Perspectives,* Alan Cobley and Alvin Thompson, eds. (Kingston: Montrose Publishers, 1990), 71.

[20] See Norman Girvan's views in the "Political Economy of Race in the Americas: The Historical Context of Garveyism," in *Garvey, His Work and Impact,* Rupert Lewis and Patrick Bryan, eds. (Kingston: ISER University of the West Indies, 1988), 11-21.

[21] Dennis Benn, *The Growth and Development of Political Ideas in the Caribbean, 1774-1983* (Kingston: ISER University of the West Indies, 1987), 135.

[22] *ibid.*

[23] Tony Martin 1984, 53.

[24] See Wilson Moses, *The Golden Age of Black Nationalism* (Hamden: Archdon Book, 1978), 16-17.

[25] Stokely Carmichael, 'Marxism Leninism,' *Black Scholar,* Vol. 4, No. 5 (February 1973), 41.

[26] E.U. Essien-Udom, *Black Nationalism: A search for an identity in America* (Chicago: Chicago University Press, 1962), 6; and James Turner, "The Sociology of Black Nationalism," *Black Schola*r, Vol. 1, No. 2 (December 1969), 18.

[27] Manning Marable, *Beyond Black and White: Transforming Afro-American Politics (London: Verso, 1995), 211-212.*

Chapter 2

[1] GH/3/5 Government House Records (Barbados Archives).

[2] See Tony Martin, *Race First* (Massachusetts: The Majority Press, 1976), 16.

[3] Interview with David Brown, 25 October 2001.

[4] GH/3/5 Government House Records (Barbados Archives).

[5] Tony Martin, *Race First*, 77.

[6] GH/3/5 Government House Records (Barbados Archives).

[7] *ibid.*

[8] *ibid*

[9] GH/37 Government House Records (Barbados Archives).

[10] *ibid.*

[11] *ibid.*

[12] See Tony Martin, *The Pan-African Connection: From slavery to Garvey and Beyond* (Massachusetts: The Majority Press, 1983), 59.

[13] GH4/38 Government House Records (Barbados Archives).

[14] GH3/5 Government House Records (Barbados Archives).

[15] Tony Martin, 13.

[16] See William Scott, *The Sons of Sheba's Race: African Americans and the Italo-Ethiopian War, 1939-1941* (Indianapolis: Indiana University Press, 1993), 6. Also see Rodney Worrell, *Pan-Africanism In the New Global Conjuncture*, 19.

[17] See S.K.B. Asante's description of the significance of this victory in Horace Campbell, *Rasta and Resistance* (London: Hansib Publishing, 1985), 50.

[18] GH/37/d Government House Records (Barbados Archives).

[19] *ibid*

[20] *ibid*

[21] *ibid.*

[22] Rupert Lewis, A Political Study of Garveyism, Jamaica and London 1914-1940. Masters Thesis. (University of the West Indies, 1971), 64.

[23] GH/37/d Government House Records (Barbados Archives).

[24] GH/38/ Government House Records (Barbados Archives).

[25] GH/37/b Government House Records (Barbados Archives).

[26] *ibid.*

[27] Tony Martim, *Race First*, 50.

[28] GH/3/5/ Government House Records (Barbados Archives).

[29] *ibid.*

[30] *ibid.*

[31] GH4/3/5 Government House Records (Barbados Archives).

[32] See "The Expulsion of Undesirables Act," March 1927.

[33] Tony Martin, *Marcus Garvey, Hero: A First Biography* (Massachusetts: The Majority Press, 1983), 76.

34 Marvin Will, "Insurrection and the Development of Political Institutions: The 1937 Rebellion and the Birth of Labour Parties and Labour Unions in Barbados," *The Journal of the Historical Society of the* Barbados Museum and Historical Society, Vol XL, 1992), 16.

35 George Belle, The Political Economy of Barbados 1937-1946. PhD Thesis (University of Manchester, 1976), 60.

36 GH 37/b Government House Records (Barbados Archives).

37 David Brown, "Barbadian Reaction to The Italian-Ethiopian War: Pan-Africanism in the Early Twentieth Century Barbados" (Seminar Paper, University of the West Indies, Cave Hill, 1988), 5.

38 GH4/37/38/d Government House Records (Barbados Archives).

39 GH 37/B Government House Records (Barbados Archives).

40 Horace Campbell, 60.

41 *ibid.*

42 Tony Martin, Race First, 236.

43 George Belle, "The Struggle for Political Democracy," in *Emancipation 111,* Alvin Thompson,ed. (History Department: University of the West Indies, Cave Hill, 1986), 62.

44 Immanuel Geiss, *The Pan-African Movement,* Anna Keep, tr. (London: Meuthen, 1974), 336.

45 GH/35 Government House Records (Barbados Archives).

46 GH/37/B Government House Records (Barbados Archives).

47 *ibid.*

48 *ibid.*

49 *ibid.*

50 *ibid.*

51 *ibid.*

52 GH4/38/d Government House Records (Barbados Archives).

53 *ibid.*

54 *ibid.*

55 David Brown, 6.

56 Tony Martin, *Race First,* 71.

57 David Brown, 6.

58 Horace Campbell, 155.

59 *ibid.,* 156.

60 David Brown, 7-8.

61 Horace Campbell, 156.

62 William Scott, xi.

63 *ibid.,* 7.

64 *ibid.*

Chapter 3

[1] See Marvin Will, "Insurrection and the Development of Political Institutions: The 1937 Rebellion and the Birth of Labour Parties in the Barbados," *The Journal of the Barbados Museum and Historical Society*, Vol. xl, 1992), 12.

[2] See Hilary Beckles, *A History of Barbados* (London: Cambridge University Press, 1990), 164.

[3] Hilary Beckles, 164.

[4] *ibid*, 165.

[5] Addington Forde, *The 1937 Disturbances of Barbados: A Summary of The Report of the Dean Commission of Enquiry* (Bridgetown, 1999), 40

[6] Tony Martin, *Race First: The Ideological and Organizational Struggles o of Marcus Garvey and the Universal Negro Improvement Association* (Massachusetts: The Majority Press), 83.

[7] Addington Forde, 41.

[8] *ibid*.

[9] Hilary Beckles, 167.

[10] *ibid*.

[11] *ibid*.

[12] *ibid*.

[13] *ibid*.

[14] *ibid*.

Chapter 4

[1] See Girvan's comment in Brian Meeks, *Caribbean Revolutions and Revolutionary Theory: An Assessment of Cuba, Nicaragua and Grenada* (Kingston: University of the West Indies Press, 1993 and 2001), 146.

[2] See Andrea King interview with Calvin Alleyne, "PPM-Party for Change," in the *Nation* (May 18, 2001).

[3] Personal Interview with Bobby Clarke (April 14, 1998). Also see "Barbadian Pioneers," *Black Star (November* 4, 1967).

[4] "Editorial," *Black Star* (November 4, 1967).

[5] Melvin Leinman, *The Political Economy of Racism: A History* (London: Pluto Press, 1993), 259.

[6] "Black Power and the Revolutionary Struggle," *Black Star* (January 11, 1969).

[7] "Blacks Must Reject Capitalism," *Black Star* (September 21, 1968).

[8] See Robert Hill, "The Restatement of Pan-Africanism," in Edward Alpers & Pierre Fontaine, *Walter Rodney Revolutionary and Scholar: A Tribute* (Los Angeles: University of California Press, 1982), 86.

[9] Frantz Fanon, *The Wretched of the Earth*, Constance Farrington, tr. Reprint. (Middlesex: Penguin, 1985), 79.

[10] Leroy Harewood, "What is to be done,"_*Black Star* (December 30, 1967).

[11] Leroy Harewood, "Adams and Co. Must Go," *Black Star* (August 3, 1968).

[12] Bob Clarke, "Socialism: Its Meaning," *Black Star* (January 27, 1968).

[13] Calvin Alleyne, "The Nature of the Struggle," *Black Star* (November 4, 1967).

[14] *ibid.*

[15] Tyrone Evelyn, "Some Problems Confronting the People," *Black Star* (December 2, 1967).

[16] *ibid.*

[17] See "Youth Speak Out,"*Black Star* (May 14, 1968).

[18] Glenroy Straughn, "On Education," *Black Star* (October 19, 1968).

[19] Walter Rodney, *The Groundings with my Brothers* (London: Bogle-L'Ouverture 1969 and 1996), 35.

[20] *ibid*, 51.

[21] Tony Martin, *Race First*, 84.

[22] Leroy Harewood, "Who are We?" *Black Star* (April 6, 1968).

[23] Leroy Harewood, "Who are We?" (2), *Black Star* (April 27, 1968).

[24] Leroy Harewood, "Who are We?" (3), *Black Star* (May 11, 1968).

[25] *ibid.*

[26] Leroy Harewood, "Who are We?' (4), *Black Star* (May 25, 1968).

[27] Ossie Redman, "The Struggle of the Masses," *Black Star* (February 10, 1968).

[28] Ava Turner, "Black Women and Beauty," *Black Star* (February 8, 1969).

[29] O.C Haynes, "We are too Slavish," *Black Star* (June 22, 1968).

[30] Tony Martin, *Race First*, 69.

[31] Frances Welsing, *The Isis Papers* (Chicago: Third World Press, 1991), 172.

[32] Ossie Redman, "Youth to Youth," *Black Star* (June 8, 1968).

[33] John Connell, "Our National Anthem," *Black Star* (November 18, 1967).

[34] *ibid.*

[35] Leroy Harewood, Shame!," *Black Star* (November 2, 1968).

[36] John Connell, "Hour of Truth," *Black Star* (November 2, 1968).

[37] Leroy Harewood, "Why Is there Underdevelopment," *Black Star* (February 8, 1969).

[38] Walter Rodney, *How Europe Under-Developed Africa* (London: Bogle L'Ouverture Publications, 1967).

[39] Frantz Fanon, 76.

[40] Leroy Harewood, "Why Is there Underdevelopment."

[41] *ibid.*

[42] "Human Rights," *Black Star* (December 14, 1968).

[43] "Che Guevara," *Black Star* (November 4, 1968).

[44] *ibid.*

[45] "Murder and Platitude," *Black Star* (March 9, 1968).

[46] "West Indians Denounce Smith-Wilson Hangings, Savage Acts of Murder," *Black Star* (March 23, 1968).

[47] "Rhodesia: Double Dealing of the West," *Black Star* (March 23, 1968.

[48] The Editorial, *Black Star*, 11 May 1968.

[49] "South Africa: Men and Money Behind Apartheid," *Black Star* (October 5, 1968).

[50] John Connell, "The Drift to the Right," *Black Star* (February 8, 1969); and "Witch Hunt hits Carib Progressives," *ibid.*

[51] *ibid.*

[52] "Meeting Held in Support of Imprisoned Students," *Black Star* (February 1969.

[53] *ibid.*

[54] "Nkrumah; Myth and Reality," *Black Star*, 2 December 1967.

[55] Nkrumah on Black Power," *Black Star* (May 11, 1968).

[56] Professor Rodney, "Jamaica Today," *Black Star* (November 16, 1968).

[57] *ibid.*

[58] *ibid.*

[59] Leroy Harewood, "This Man Must Go," *Black Star* (July 20, 1968); and "Budget Shoots at Black Star," *ibid.*

[60] Editorial, "Democracy," *Black Star* (May 24, 1969).

[61] "A vote to Break Their Own Necks," *Black Star* (May 24, 1969).

[62] Andrea King, "PPM-Party for Change," *Nation* (May 18, 2001).

[63] Clarence Munford, *Race and Reparations: A black Perspective for the 21st Century* (Trenton: African World Press, 1996), 152.

[64] Personal Interview with Bobby Clarke. Also see Rodney Worrell, *Pan-Africanism in Barbados*, in Glenford Howe& Don Marshall, the Empowering Impulse: The Nationalist Tradition of Barbados (Kingston: University of the West Indies Press, 2001), 210; and "The Public Order

Act," 1970.

[65] Andrea King.

[66] The House of Assembly Debates (May 12, 1970).

[67] *ibid.*

[68] *ibid.*

Chapter 5

[1] Elton Mottley, "Black Night Role in Idea," *Advocate* (July 18, 1970).

[2] Elton Mottley, "Imported Ideology, but It's Relevant," *Advocate* (July 15, 1970); Elton Mottley, "What the Idea Means," *Advocate* (July 16, 1970).

[3] Walter Rodney, *The Groundings with My Brothers* (London: Bugle-L'Ouverture Publications, 1969), 28.

[4] See Stokely Carmichael and Charles Hamilton, *Black Power: The Politics of Liberation* (Middlessex: Penguin Books, 1967), 58-59; and "We Are all Africans," *The Black Scholar*, Vol. 1, No. 7 (May 1970), 15.

[5] Elton Mottley, "What the Idea Means."

[6] *ibid.*

[7] Manning Marable, *Race Reform and Rebellion–The Second Reconstruction in Black America 1945-1982* (London: MacMillian Press, 1984), 107; and Harold Cruse, *Rebellion or Revolutions* (New York: William and Morrow, 1968), 207. Also see Rodney Worrell, *Pan-Africanism in the New Global Conjuncture* (Miami, Florida: Universal Publishers, 2003).

[8] Interview with Kofi Akobi (September 12, 1998). Also see Rodney Worrell, "Pan-Africanism in Barbados," 210.

[9] *Southern African Liberation Committee Information Bulletin* (September 1980).

[10] See Amilcar Cabral, *Revolution in Guinea: An African Peoples Struggle* (London: Stage 1, 1974), 65-66.

[11] Southern African Liberation Committee, *Sports and Apartheid* (Bridgetown, 1993).

[12] "Help Those in S. Africa," *Advocate*, (March 25, 1983).

[13] SALC Files, Press Release, (June 8, 1982).

[14] Michael Cummins, "SALC Calls on Community to Fight Apartheid, Fascism," *Advocate* (July 9, 1981).

[15] Southern African Liberation Committee Files, (February 15, 1982).

[16] Southern African Liberation Committee, Space Research Corp. (Bridgetown, 1981).

[17] *ibid.*, 13.

[18] SALC Press Release, "SALC Backs Guyana Move" (March 7, 1981).
[19] *ibid.*
[20] *ibid.*
[21] *ibid.*
[22] *ibid.*
[23] SALC Files, "The Robin Jackman Affair"(Press Release, March 7, 1981); "SALC Protest outside BHC," *Advocate* (March 15, 1981).
[24] SALC Press Release (March 8, 1982).
[25] *ibid.*
[26] *ibid.*
[27] SALC Files, *Sports and Apartheid*, 22.
[28] SALC Files (January 19, 1983).
[29] "Cricketers Who Turned down Appeal Praised," *Advocate* (April 24, 1983).
[30] "Denounce New Zealand's Decision Says SALC," *Advocate* (July 28, 1981).
[31] Ronald Walters, *Pan-Africanism in the African Diaspora: An Analysis of Modern Afrocentric Political Movements* (Detroit: Wayne State University Press, 1993), 299.
[32] Horace Campbell, *Rasta and Resistance: From Marcus Garvey to Walter Rodney* (London: Hansib Publication, 1985), 173.
[33] Lloyd Jones, Interview with author (September 3, 1998); David Commissiong, Interview with author (September 12, 1998).
[34] Interview with David Commissiong.
[35] "Cadogan to run in St. Peter," *Nation,* (April 6, 1986).
[36] Voice of the Clement Payne Movement, *Black Liberation Days.*
[37] Interview with David Commissiong, Interview with David Denny.
[38] See Max Stafford, "The Pan-African Party," *The Black Scholar*, Vol. 2. No. 6 (February 1971), 27.
[39] "Commissiong to Blow Own Trumphet," *Pulse* (September 11-17, 1992).
[40] *ibid.*
[41] Leroy Harewood, "The Commissiong–Haynes Alliance: Will It Work?," *Pulse* (September 25 – October 1, 1992).
[42] "Time for Reform," *Nation* (June 2, 1993).
[43] The 1994 NDP Manifesto, 13.
[44] Julius Gittens, "Democracy Myth Blown Up," *Sunday Sun* (May 20, 1993).
[45] 1994 Manifesto of the National Democratic Party, 13.
[46] See Naiwu Oshanon, "The Call," Pan-African Foundation of Lagos,

PAMOB Files.

[47] See the Constitution of the Pan-African Movement of Barbados.

[48] See Editorial, *New Vision*, Vol. 1, No. 1 (July 1991).

[49] Olutoye Walrond, "PAMOB Congratulated," *New Vision*, Vol. 1, No. 2 (1991).

[50] Leroy Harewood, "New Vision, We're Here to Chart a New Path," *New Vision*, Vol. 1, No. 1 (July 1991).

[51] PAMOB Files.

[52] *ibid.*

[53] PAMOB Files and Ikael Tafari, "Pan-African Organizations Meet," *Carribbean Contact*, Vol. 18, No. 8 (September/October 1991).

[54] *ibid.*

[55] See Commission for Pan-African Affairs Brochure.

[56] *ibid.*

Bibliography

Abdul, Raheem Tajudeen. *Pan-Africanism: Politics, Economy and Social Change in the Twenty-First Century*. New York: New York University Press, 1996

Alpers, Edward and Pierre Fontaine. *Walter Rodney Revolutionary and Scholar: A Tribute*. Los Angeles: University of California Press, 1982

Beckles, Hilary. *A History of Barbados*. London: Cambridge University Press, 1990

Belle, George. The Political Economy of Barbados 1937-1946. PHD Dissertation: University of Manchester, 1976

Benn, Dennis. *The Growth and Development of Political Ideas in the Caribbean 1774-1983*. Kingston: ISER University of the West Indies, 1987

Brown, David. *Barbadian Reactions to the Italian-Ethiopian War: Pan-Africanism in the Early Twentieth Century Barbados*. Seminar Paper. Cave Hill: University of the West Indies, 1988

Cabral, Amilcar. *Revolution in Guinea: An African Peoples Struggle*. London: Stage 1, 1974

Campbell, Horace. *Rasta and Resistance: From Marcus Garvey to Walter Rodney*. London: Hansib Publishing, 1985

Carmichael, Stokely and Charles Hamilton. *Black Power: The Politics of Liberation in America*. New York: Random House, 1967

Cobley, Alan and Alvin Thompson. *The African Caribbean Connection, Historical and Cultural Perspectives*. Kingston: Montrose Publishers, 1990

Cruse, Harold. *Rebellion or Revolutions*. New York: William Morrow, 1968

Duncan, Neville. "Movements as Sub-Cultures: A Preliminary Examination of Social and Political Movements in the Anglophone Caribbean" (unpublished pamphlet), 1983

Esedebe, P.Olisuwuche. *Pan-Africanism*. Cambridge, MA: Harvard University Press, 1983

Essien-Udom, E.U. *Black Nationalism: A search for an identity in America*. Chicago: Chicago University Press, 1962

Forde, Addington. *The 1937 Disturbances of Barbados: A Summary of the Report of the Dean Commission of Enquiry*. Bridgetown: Self-Published, 1999

Fanon, Frantz. *The Wretched of the Earth*. Translated by Constance Farrington. Reprint, Middlesex: Penguin, 1985

Geiss, Immanuel. *The Pan-African Movement*. Translated by Anna Keep. London: Methuen, 1962

Gray, Obika. *Radicalism and Social Change in Jamaica, 1960-1972*. Knoxville: The University of Tennesse Press, 1991

Gutkind, Peter and Immanuel Wallerstein. *The Political Economy of Contemporary Africa*. California: Sage Publications, 1976

Howe, Glenford and Don Marshall. *The Empowering Impulse: The Nationalist Tradition of Barbados*. Kingston: University of the West Indies Press, 2001

James, C.L.R. *At the Rendevous of victory*. London: Alison and Busby, 1984

Legum, Colin. *Pan-Africanism: A Short Political Guide*. London: Pall Mall Press, 1962

Leinman, Melvin. *The Political Economy of Racism: A history*. London: Luton Press, 1993

Lewis, Rupert. A Political Study of Garveyism, Jamaica and London 1914-1940. Masters thesis. Mona: University of the West Indies, 1971

Marable, Manning. *Race Reform and Rebellion: The Second Reconstruction in Black America 1945-1982*. London: MacMillian Press, 1984

_____. *Beyond Black and White: Transforming Afro-American Politics*. London: Verso, 1995

Martin, Tony. *Marcus Garvey, Hero: A First Biography*. Dover, Massachusetts: The Majority Press, 1983

_____. *The Pan-African Connection, from Slavery to Garvey and Beyond*. Dover, Massachusetts: The Majority Press, 1984

_____. *Race First: The Ideological and Organizational Struggles of Marcus Garvey and the Universal Negro Improvement Association*. London: Greenwood Press, 1976

Meeks, Brian. *Caribbean Revolutions and Revolutionary Theory: An Assessment of Cuba, Nicaragua and Grenada*. Kingston: University of the West Indies Press, 2001

Moses, Wilson. *The Golden Age of Black Nationalism*. Hamden: Archdon Book, 1978

Munford, Clarence. *Race and Reparations: A black Perspective for the 21st Century*. Trenton: African World Press, 1970

Rodney, Walter. *The Groundings with my Brothers*. London: Bougle-L'Ouverture, 1969

_____. *How Europe Under-Developed Africa*. London: Bougle-L'Ouverture, 1972

Ryan, Selwyn and Taimoo Stewart. *The Black Power Revolution 1970: A Retrospective*. The University of the West Indies, St Augustine: ISER, 1995

Rude, George. *Ideology and Popular Protest*. New York: Pantheon Books, 1980

Rush, Gary and Serge R. Denisoff. *Social and Political Movements*. New York: Meredith Corporation, 1971

Scott, William. *The Sons of Sheba's Race: African Americans and the Italo-Ethiopian War, 1939-1941*. Bloomington, IN: Indiana University Press, 1993

Stein, Judith. *The World of Marcus Garvey: Race and Class in Modern Society*. Baton Rouge: Louisiana State University Press, 1986

Thompson, Alvin. *Emancipation 111*. Cave Hill: University of the West Indies, 1988

Walters, Ronald. *Pan-Africanism in the African Diaspora: An Analysis of Modern Afro-Centric Political Movements*. Detroit: Wayne State University, 1993

Wallerstein, Immanuel. *The Capitalist World Economy*. London: Cambridge University Press, 1979

Welsing, Frances. *The Isis Papers*. Chicago: Third World Press, 1991

Will, Marvin. "Insurrection and the Development of Political Institutions: The 1937 Rebellion and the Birth of Labour Parties and Labour Unions in Barbados," *The Journal of the Historical Society of Barbados*, Vol. XL, 1992

Worrell, Rodney. *Pan-Africanism in the New Global Conjuncture: Has the Internationalization of Capital Rendered This Concept Irrelevant*. M.Phil. thesis. Cave Hill: University of the West Indies, 1999

Newspapers, journals
Advocate
Black Scholar
Black Star

Caribbean Contact
Nation
New Vision
Pulse

Other references
"Expulsion of the Undesirables Act," March 1937
Government House Records, Barbados Archives
House of Assembly Debates (May 12, 1970)
"Manifesto of the National Democratic Party," 1994
Pan-African Movement of Barbados Files (August 31, 1998)
"Personal Interview with Bobby Clarke," Bridgetown, Barbados (April 14, 1998)
"Personal Interview with David Commissiong," Bridgetown, Barbados (September 15, 1998)
"Personal Interview with David Denny," Bridgetown, Barbados (February 10, 2001)
"Personal Interview with Glenroy Straughn," Bridgetown, Barbados (June 16, 2001)
"Personal Interview with Kofi Akobi," Bridgetown, Barbados (September 12, 1998)
"Personal Interview with Lloyd Jones," Bridgetown, Barbados (September 3, 1998)
"Personal Interview with Ricky Parris," Bridgetown, Barbados (August 24, 1998)
Southern African Liberation Committee. Space Research Corp. Bridgetown: Southern Africa Liberation Committee, 1981
Southern African Liberation Committee Information Bulletin, (September-October 1980)
Southern African Liberation files. Press Release (June 8, 1982)

www.ingramcontent.com/pod-product-compliance
Lightning Source LLC
Chambersburg PA
CBHW022112280326
41933CB00007B/357